PRAISE FOR LYNETTE AND THE SEVEN SENSES OF LEADERSHIP

What an enjoyable and impactful read! Lynette Louise has done it again with *The Seven Senses of Leadership: The Brain Broad's Guide To Leadership Sensitivities.* The book is insightful, witty and a must read if you want to lead yourself and others into success. Tapping into her own life experiences from working in the field of Neurofeedback, being a mother of 8 and her incredible ground breaking work in the field of autism, this book doesn't just talk about leadership, it exemplifies it.

A great read for anyone who is already in a leadership role or aspiring to be.

Patrick Bertagna, Serial Entrepreneur Chairman and CEO of GTX Corp (GTXO) makers of the award winning Smart Sole.

Lynette Louise, also known as The Brain Broad, demonstrates her mastery of brain potential and leadership capabilities in her groundbreaking book, *The Seven Senses of Leadership.* Lynette uses a creative blend of science, examples of well-known leaders, and humor to educate and inspire people to create their own definition of leadership based on their beliefs and purpose---and then shows them how to step into the role. Anyone who wants to feel vibrantly alive will benefit immensely from reading this book! Also, I believe this should be required reading for any politician.

Sharkie Zartman. All American Professional Athlete, Award Winning Coach, Author, Speaker, Health Professor, and Radio Host of Sharkie's Pep Talk

Lynette Louise' book *The Seven Senses of Leadership* is an EYE OPENER.

She gently leads a horse to water, invites you to smell the roses, taste the bitter and the sweet. Lynette, The Brain Broad, simply shares with you, the ways in which, all the secrets to being a successful leader...or person... exist in the world around you.

STOP! TAKE TIME TO READ THE *7 Senses!*

It's more than just common sense, its common sense made common.

Kenny Robinson, Winner of the Phil Hartman Award,
Gemini Nominated Comedy Writer/ Mentor, Creator/Host
'After Hours With Kenny Robinson'

What does the brain have to do with leadership? Everything. Brain and behavior expert Lynette Louise brilliantly crafted a guidebook on what it really means to be a leader and how to implement effective leadership systems. Her ideology is applicable to any business size or level. The book is inspiring and poignant.

Amy Jordan, Dancer with the Stars, Motivational Speaker/Leader
for Diabetics and Trauma Victims who Lose Limbs, Founder & Artistic
Director of: The Victory Dance Project

Lynette's business acumen is extraordinary. Her drive to succeed, exemplary. Still, the story doesn't end there. Her deep sensitivities toward uplifting others through her own skills is the key to her writing success. In her book *The Seven Senses of Leadership*, Lynette teaches us that one of the marks of true leadership is the courage of having lead ourselves from the darkness into the fresh air of serving others with our light! Thank you Lynette.

Al Cole creator of the Humanitarian Awards from CBS Radio
and Host of the syndicated talk show "People of Distinction"
Author of "The Spirit of Romance!

The Seven Senses of Leadership is the book you've been waiting for. It dispels myths, gives you the scientific facts, helps you to understand the biology of leadership and gives you strategies to be better. Lynette is the definition of a Leader; in her field of Neurofeedback, in life, in motherhood and as a pioneer in the treatment of Autism. This book is filled with Lynette's unique perspective, infectious humor, passion, deep knowledge and extensive research. The result is the most beautiful distillation of wisdom – her very own, unique Scent of Leadership. I couldn't put it down and read it from cover to cover in one day. The

Seven Senses of Leadership is a book every Leader should read, re-read and share.

Elisabetta L Faenza, Master of International Relations,
Master of Education, Corporate Profiler, Best-selling Author/Speaker

Lynette Louise has an innate ability to reach and relate to people of all ages and backgrounds. She succeeds with major breakthroughs. Her results are unprecedented. It is her ability to tune in and relate to people. Traveling the globe she is sought out for her breakthrough methods that work that change people's lives. She helps everyone better understand how they think and relate to people by better understanding their brain. *The Seven Senses of Leadership* is both thought provoking and inspiring. This book will inform your understanding of how and why you must love to lead if you wish to lead with love. Lynette is amazing in every aspect of her work. From authoring books to being an amazing speaker on stage with humor, passion and compassion."

Sharon A. Burstein, President / CEO, Sharon Burstein International
Award-winning author, Speaker, International Leadership
and Marketing Consultant

Thank you Lynette for sharing your passion and courage at our Mending Hearts Gala. You brought the crowd to their feet with your story of determination and perseverance and helped Yellow Brick House raise crucial funds for our Crisis line.

If you're ready to experience more joy and happiness, then hire my friend Lynette Louise as she truly cares about making a positive difference!"

To Hire Lynette Louise as a Speaker or Show Guest
www.lynettelouise.com

THE SEVEN SENSES OF LEADERSHIP

The Brain Broad's Guide to Leadership Sensibilities

LYNETTE LOUISE

MOtivational PRESS

LEADERS IN GLOBAL PUBLISHING

Published by Motivational Press, Inc.
1777 Aurora Road
Melbourne, Florida, 32935
www.MotivationalPress.com

Manufactured in the United States of America.

ISBN: 978-1-62865-322-9

CONTENTS

"Leadership is, most fundamentally, about the power of influence. What leaders do is influence people, empower and elevate them up to a whole new level or change in some creative ways to take advantage of new opportunities."

Hon. Tamer Hegazy,
Global Minister of Entrepreneurship

In April of 2015 a group of terrorists – equipped with special bullets– ambushed the UN's motorcade in Somalia. The bulletproofing was no longer effective and Hon. Tamer Hegazy was shot over 30 times. As the bullets tore into the car he and his security detail suffered severe injuries. His driver, as well as nine others, died. He remains dedicated to serving through leadership, knocking down barriers and empowering global health.

FOREWORD

Leadership is about influence—the ability to influence people. Without influence, it is impossible to be a leader. Viewing leadership as a process means that leaders affect and are effected by their followers, either positively or negatively. Leadership is a two-way, interactive event between leaders and followers rather than a linear, one-way event in which the leader only affects the followers.

The Seven Senses of Leadership: The Brain Broad's Guide to Leadership Sensibilities is a book that honors this relationship and gives us knowledge of our already existing influence, allowing us to become effective leaders and followers.

We have influence and can affect others' beliefs, attitudes, and behavior. This book focuses on personal power. It explains how to attain personal power with its capacity to influence. *The Seven Senses of Leadership: The Brain Broad's Guide to Leadership Sensibilities* teaches the way in which personal power is derived from the development of interpersonal relationships that all leaders develop with followers. This book is important.

Today's leadership capacity is insufficient to meet future leadership requirements. Leaders are not adequately prepared for the future. The four most important future skills—leading people, strategic planning, inspiring commitment, and managing change—are among the weakest competencies for today's leaders. The leadership gap, then, appears notably in high-priority, high-stakes areas. There is a significant gap between the needed and existing skill levels in employee development, balancing personal life and work, and decisiveness.

A leadership gap or deficit may have one of two causes: when leaders are focused on the right competencies but haven't sufficiently mastered them, or when leaders are not focused on the right skill areas.

The book between your hands outlines notable trends in the personal acquisition of leadership senses and development; offers insights that are necessary for our future.

In the past two decades, such trends included the proliferation of new leadership development methods and a growing recognition of the importance of a leader's emotional resonance with others. A growing recognition that leadership development involves more than just developing individual leaders has now led to a greater focus on the context in which leadership is developed, thoughtful consideration about how to best use leadership competencies, personal intelligence and work/life balance issues.

After reading this book *The Seven Senses of Leadership: The Brain Broad's Guide to Leadership Sensibilities* seven of your senses are going to be impacted. These are the seven senses most consistently viewed as ultimately important in the attainment of quality leadership skills, now and in the future. They are: leading people, strategic planning, inspiring commitment, managing change, resourcefulness, being a quick learner, and doing whatever it takes.

Take my word for it; this book is all about what you need, and don't have, when it comes to leadership talent; equally to emergent and assigned leadership. The next pages come with rich content able to enforce the leader's ability to inspire confidence and support among people seeking to achieve goals.

This book will help you harness and understand your influence using the tools you already have, your seven senses of leadership.

H.E Tamer Hegazy
Global Minister of Entrepreneurship

ACKNOWLEDGMENTS

In general I hesitate to write acknowledgments because it is impossible to actually mention everyone that deserves a thank you. The truth is my life has been moved forward in the arms of others, and as such I could fill a book with gratitude. I have been able to live a remarkable story, and many have contributed to the knowledge I share in this book. So, thank you everyone, especially my children. However, though there have been too many to name, there are a few people that I absolutely have to mention because this book required their brilliance, cooperation, and excellence.

In order of contributing efforts: Rachel Clark for transcribing my spoken word. Tsara Shelton for making my spoken word readable. Ma'ayan Cohen for fact checking with great attention to detail. Cleone Reed for a loving edit that maintains my voice. And not to forget, the designers and formatters at motivational press as well as Justin Sachs, my publisher, and his team, especially Tom Matkovic for putting up with my careful and constant revisions.

My appreciation for, and admiration to, you all.

For Dar,

My Teacher

PREFACE

MYTHS: Leaders are highly educated college graduates. Leaders are high school dropout students. Leaders are politicians, marketers, liars, truth-tellers, celebrities, businessmen, teachers, lawyers, popes and monks on mountains. They are exhibitionists in the spotlight and always on. They take the time to analyze and choose and delegate while leading from behind the curtain. They are the puppeteers, the performers, the silent but watching. They are visionaries. They are grounded in reality. They are men. They are women. They are old. They are young. They are alive. They are dead. They are Leaders and Leaders Lead.

There are many **Myths** about what it takes to be a Leader. Throughout this book I will highlight and dispel a few of them. One thing is certain. If you are using the adjective Leader that person is Leading, someone.

What Makes a Leader's Brain? The answer to this question is unknown. Science has learned more about the brain in the last fifteen years than it had in all the centuries before rolled into one. However, despite the volumes of newly acquired knowledge and man's advances in imaging technology, the world of science still knows next to nothing about what makes a Leader's brain tick. Is it education? Hardship? Breeding? Luck? Stubbornness? Narcissism? I.Q? Or is it the silver spoon of opportunity?

None of these, and all of these, has contributed to the great, big and small, Leader stories throughout history.

Chris Gardner was a homeless father with a toddler in tow (1980's) who became a stockbroker millionaire, author, and producer of his own story (Gardner, 2006). Albert Einstein 1879–1955 with an estimated I.Q. of 160 developed the general theory of relativity—a pillar of modern physics—and is a historically renowned scientist that used his intellect to change the course of history (Idsiach, 2006). Cynthia Stafford was a struggling mom caring for five children when she won 112 Million dollars in 2007 and became known as one of Los Angeles' biggest philanthropists (Upfromsplatcom, 2010).

In the early 1980's a confident Tony Robbins claimed he could correct a stranger's phobia within minutes on live Radio, Stage and TV, then he did. British monarch Queen Victoria born 1819 crowned 1837–1901 lent her name to The Victorian Era and increased the size of her kingdom many fold during her exceptionally long reign (Eric Evans, 2011).

FACT: ALL LEADERS HAVE A DIFFERENT BRAIN.

The brain is magnificent whether used to Lead others or not. And when it is working at full capacity it consumes vast stores of our energy. For example, it eats up 20% of our oxygen intake, 25% of our glucose and oodles of our cardiac output (Rensburg, 2012). It uses all that fuel just to think and man the controls of our actions. Some theorists say a Leader's brain uses less energy than the average man's because Leaders are more efficient thinkers. Maybe. However, other theorists have hypothesized that a Leader's constant drive to learn new knowledge and reach new horizons actually consumes more energy than is typical. This is said to be because that hunger for more keeps the Leader's brain in a constant state of construction.

These are both true. All brains—Leaders and non-Leaders alike—are always under construction. All brains—Leaders and non-Leaders alike—become more efficient through repetition. So doing what you do on a consistent basis, even if what you do is Lead, leads to a form of efficiency.

Therefore, despite this three-pound organ's minute size, its 100 billion neurons still have scientists guessing and arguing about function. There is no answer on the subject of how a Leader's brain is constructed. And this land of scientific uncertainty has bred many myths, accidental truths, and mistaken assumptions. However, though we can't understand how a Leader's brain functions we *can* observe how a Leader behaves: As long as we agree on the definition of "Leader."

But we don't.

SO, DEFINING OUR DEFINITIONS IS THE PLACE TO BEGIN.

Great Leaders, like great spouses, match us. Therefore there is no definitive universally correct descriptive for *"Leader."* You will have to create your own definition. This book will help you with that. Right now!

And once you understand your definition you will be able to step into it if you so choose. So let's begin.

Ask yourself, "Who is a great leader?" and follow the answer to find your beliefs. You cannot be wrong, though you may be surprised.

GREAT LEADERS AREN'T LIMITED TO ANY ARENA OF ENDEAVOR.

They aren't all introverted peace revolutionaries like *Mahatma Gandhi who despite his self-reflective nature was the political Leader of the Indian independence movement in the 1940's* (Sowards, 1995). Neither are they all rich industrial Leaders like *Henry Ford who in the early 1900's optimized automobile production with the installation of assembly lines and effectively grew an empire by making things more efficient.* Some Leaders create and some simply reinvent in order to market. *According to Steve Jobs—unarguably a leader—"Picasso had a saying—'Good Artists Copy; Great Artists Steal"* (Isaacson, 2015). I am not sure if he thought of artists as Leaders, but I do know that some Leaders simply build upon and bring life to the ideas of others.

Like the brain and its sensory system, nothing happens in isolation, not even Leadership. All human positioning is done from within the network of life, the expectations, beliefs, and actions, of others and of ourselves.

One December day in 1955 Rosa Parks (born 1914) sat on a bus and refused to move even though a white woman wanted her seat. The response to her refusal and the actions of the people around her, including others who had similarly refused to give up their seats, led to a boycott that helped bring about the end of segregation in the public facilities of America (Congress, 2010). If she had not been arrested, if no one paid attention to her refusal or if she had faltered in her Leadership, it is possible that the movement would not have happened. Leaders lead others who follow.

How will you recognize your Leader? The one you wish to be or follow? What is your definition?

I don't know. That is for you to answer but I will tell you mine.

Lynette's Leader Belief: A Leader's desire to act is in touch with their core purpose and remains the same throughout their life. For this reason, despite all the self-development and learning, all the adventures and accomplishments, Leaders can look back over their entire life and see the thread of sameness in the reasons for their actions. This sameness also creates congruence in the picture that we see. They are steadfast.

> *"Happiness Is When, What You Think, What You Say, And What You Do Are In Harmony."*
> *Mahatma Gandhi*
> *(Kirov, 2014)*

Leaders know what they want to be and are driven to be it.

LET'S TALK ABOUT perSEEving

Too often, people divide the brain into either *psychology* or *physiology* in order to explain something and pass on a concept. For example, a

Preface

typical statement by many is, "Seeing is believing." And they are right. But on occasion their listeners—who will likely be *seen* as deep thinkers—may flip that around and say "Believing is seeing." And they are also

> *"Whether You Think You Can, Or You Think You Can't—You're Right."*
>
> Henry Ford (Jeremy, 2006)

right. These "deep thinkers" may even raise an eyebrow with a sardonic "Touché" expression while slapping their conversational opponents using the imaginary glove of competition. Suddenly, the cooperative state of listener and speaker is dissolved and the age-old fight of *mind or matter* begins, again. This dance of distraction happens, with regularity, all over the world.

Don't Dance: The *mind or matter* argument proliferates competition to prevent progression.

In fact, they are both right and equally as deep.

SEEING DOES LEAD TO BELIEVING *AND* BELIEVING DOES LEAD TO SEEING.

They work together and build upon each other.

This may sound confusing. But give me a minute to explain. It's the act of believing (or expecting) that causes your brain to choose what bits and pieces, out of the landscape of possibilities in front of you, that you will perSEEv. And it's the bits and pieces that you SEE that substantiate and inform you on what to BELIEVE. Hence you perSEEv the world around you. And you perSEEv it through the cooperative functioning of believing AND seeing.

SO GO AHEAD. BELIEVE WHAT YOU SEE AND YOU WILL SEE WHAT YOU BELIEVE!

All sensory perceptions work this way. They communicate in an

18

inescapable feedback loop of creation wherein your *physiology* and your *psychology* work together to build a constantly growing version of YOUR individual truth (Wagner and Silber, 2004).

Thus, since this perpetual gerbil wheel of "create and recreate" is true for all your senses, there can be no absolute position of correctness. We can never know it all, or even each other, with completeness. We can, however, know ourselves, moment to moment, second to second, and belief to belief.

If you wish to hone your *Leadership Sensibilities,* you must understand how perfect it is that all things are in a state of flux. This truth gives you freedom from the need to be perfect. You cannot get it right and then stick to that because there is no permanent right. Thus you, the Leader, must always and forever be evolving, ahead of the curve, and worthy of notice, aka of being perSEEved.

To explain these sensory feedback loops of Leading others I have divided this book into the Seven Senses of Leadership.

However, though we will begin with SIGHT, remember that SEEing is only the beginning of this book and is *not* necessarily the beginning of perception itself.

So to be clear (because thinking on so many fronts can be confusing) I will restate the concept:

Perceiving, spelled, "perSEEving," is wholly done via not just the physiology of your eyes and brain, (Brown, 2012) but also via the physiology of every one of your senses mingled with each other *and* the psychology you consciously and subconsciously apply to each and every bit of information coming in through these channels.

Therefore the idea of *Leadership Sensibilities* is based on an understanding of how the creation of a Leader is built out of the chaos of sensory input (Kenny and Fraser, 2012). *Leadership Sensibilities* **does not** refer to having delicate sensitivities, and definitely **does not** imply weakness in the heart of a Leader, for that would be a conceptual oxymoron. Weak Leaders are *fake* Leaders scaring their followers into submission or passive aggressively asking for support and handouts. Understand that a passive-aggressive leader is not a leader of souls, but a shackler of loyalties.

LEADERS CHOOSE STRENGTH AND SET THEIR FOLLOWERS FREE. IN FACT, THEY INSIST UPON IT.

To be a Leader, strength is a necessary component, because a Leader must be comparatively stronger than at least one other soul, whom they then Lead into growing stronger as well.

Leaders Lead others into states of independence. They do this—in part—in order to free themselves from the shackles of their followers. Leaders Lead. And they thrive on challenge. That is why they must free themselves, so that they can search for bigger challenges with more people in need of their guidance. Leaders Lead and then let go, in order to grow.

Leaders, like parents, must always be moving towards a state of separation from their followers. The student becomes a peer and eventually surpasses the teacher that knew well how to Lead. To do that Leaders will push themselves toward a goal, modeling success and exampling independent action, growing increasingly more capable through the life experience presented to them on their wheel of reinvention. This nonstop action results in unstoppable forward momentum.

This is what *Leadership Sensibilities* imply. Growth. And though it is true that Leaders are sensitive, their sensitivities are extended to their followers, and not about themselves. Leaders are too busy Leading to be easily waylaid, offended, or shocked.

In a sound bite: ***Leaders Lead without Apology!***

If you are a natural-born Leader you already recognize these things in yourself because you have always Led, someone.

This book will help you refine and perfect your skills by helping you understand how you are doing it.

If, however, you only wish you were a Leader and are reading because you want to cultivate Leadership skills, be encouraged; in many ways it is easy.

Simply start Leading, someone. Then, using this book and your *Seven Senses* to observe and create yourself and others anew, you too will learn how to refine and perfect yourself while you grow your audience.

When you intend on helping others in a way that builds your strength, the interplay between experience and desire will reshape your physiology and you will become more adept at it, no matter where you are on the learning curve. You will grow your *Leadership Sensibilities* simply by understanding how!

Intentional growth that results in the desired skill sets is always more successfully undergone when people are fully informed on the tools they will be (or maybe already are) working with. Thus, understanding how your senses shape you is imperative for purposely improving as a Leader. That is where this book comes in.

The Seven Senses of Leadership reveals your tools and tells you how you should and/or do use them. This information is shared through, and about, the very feedback loops with which you learn and create, thereby teaching you how you can, and do, invent yourself. So be a Leader (or follower), but be it with awareness via an understanding of your own beliefs and sensibilities.

Yes, believing *is* **Seeing**. But it is also **Hearing** and **Smelling** and **Tasting** and **Feeling** and **Balancing** and, even, **Leading**.

For these are **The Seven Senses of Leadership** that comprise your *Leadership Sensibility.*

MYTH #1

Once a Leader always a Leader!

It is possible to be a Leader once, decide it sucks, and do something else.

William Shakespeare coined the phrase, "Some are born great, some achieve greatness, and some have greatness thrust upon them," in the early 1600's (Greaves, 2003). This line from the play "Twelfth Night" was so intrinsically resonant with humans that it is even entrenched in popular speech today. It has evolved as a saying reinforcing the possibility of changing your destiny.

MYTHS like "Leaders are born not made" imply a static, fated position for man in the adventure of life. It is possible that people and organizations propagate these ideas in order to build an army of blind obedience. It is possible that this is done in an attempt to maintain superiority and productivity by keeping others in their station. But ideas don't grow simply because they have been planted. They must fall on fertile soil. Ideas like these get a foothold when the believer sees a benefit to nurturing their growth. However, though this type of believing can be used as an excuse to give up and let your mind and body atrophy, most people crave to improve, so it is only when people are emotionally overwhelmed and unable to sift through the garbage of yellow journalism that the fertile soil for mental manipulation exists. This is because beliefs about the absence of human choice are generally resisted out of instinct. And they should be. After all, what would be the point of education, of teaching our children, if we did not believe that skills—even the skills of Leadership—can be learned?

Parents of multiple offspring know the answer; and if they don't, they should.

Most parents of more than one child long ago discovered that all children learn, albeit at their own pace. They also solved the *nature versus nurture* conundrum when their second baby, who arrived fresh from the womb personality intact, began interacting with the family. The new child immediately pursued both sameness and oppositeness with various family members, most especially the sibling closest to him or her. For the parents watching their child's immersion identity dance, it should become obvious that infants start out with a core personality, then adapt and recreate as they live alongside others.

Everyone switches from follower to Leader and Leader to follower under the right circumstances and with the right influences. Husbands can dominate at work but kowtow to their wives at home. Wives can be strong with their children and weak with their mothers. Even animals are known to switch places, one moment being the alpha dog, the next moment cowering with their tail between their legs. But for people there is something else to consider. In addition to this typical evolutionary dance of swaying within the bipolar bongo beat of being human, people can appear to be rocked out of their chosen core state.

Emotional crisis, physical trauma, addiction and/or disease can change the brain (Zillmer, Spiers, and Culbertson, 2007) and make a Leader seem subservient or force a follower to Lead.

Often the change is triggered by something so monumental that Leaders lose touch with their passion and give up on their life's mission. Sometimes an event brings out the follower's deepest sense of responsibility and propels them to Lead, possibly even for the rest of their lives. Yet, though the actions, moods and cognitions have changed, the core person stays the same. All choices are made from the core and no life is devoid of choices. No matter how the pendulum swings to evolve the person, they will always be themselves, colored by change, recognizable, though different, day upon day, deed upon deed, decade upon decade.

Some people further confuse understanding this by having a personality-passion-core based on flexibility. These people rise up to Lead on opposing platforms for some period in their life and then fall back behind the lines for another. They often do this more than once, all while staying true to their core of shifting states.

Hence life is confusing when you want to believe just one thing: "People never change!" or "Everybody changes!"

In fact it is, as you believe it to be, for you. But regardless of your beliefs, no one and nothing is stagnant, even though it all stays the same, while changing.

Think of your core like a category of music. Rock! The *rock* stays the same but the songs constantly change. Be aware though. Not everyone is so easy to categorize because some have a core of eclectic musical tastes.

"Some are born great, some achieve greatness, and some have greatness thrust upon them," resonates when we think about changing states, but it becomes more inclusive when something other than greatness is being discussed. Not everyone thinks greatness is a worthy goal, nor believes in change. Additionally, the definition of "greatness" like the definition of "Leader" fluctuates within the rhythm of time, culture, economics, and personal taste.

So though you may start out as a Leader and end as a follower, or start as a follower and end as a Leader, you will have always been the same, even as you grew different. This is good news! It means that the possibilities are limitless because nothing is stagnant. This is also good news because the fear of losing yourself in the process is without reason, since regardless of the changes you stay the same.

To be clear: You don't become someone else! You don't change your core! But you do rewire and construct pathways! So you do change. You change your ability to perSEEv and eventually to function within a new reality.

|||||||||||||||||||||||||||||||||||||||||||||| ▼ ▼ ▼ |||||||||||||||||||||||||||||||||||||||||||||||||

LEADER: OSKAR SCHINDLER (1908–1974) is an interesting choice as a Leader example. He is the subject of the Steven Spielberg movie *Schindler's List* with Liam Neeson and was a German industrialist spy, a member of the Nazi party, who amassed a fortune by using Jews for cheap labor and then spent it all to save the very race he was exploiting. Schindler's List refers to the names of the 1,200 Jews he saved during the Holocaust (Byers, 2005).

Oskar Schindler is an apparent enigma and has been labeled an opportunist by many. His story is littered with risky business, some successes, more failures, wives, mistresses, legitimate as well as illegitimate offspring, subterfuge, and danger. Schindler himself estimated his wartime (1942–1945) acquisitions and expenditures (including bribes and relocations costs) related to saving Jews at $1,056,000 (a huge amount of money for that period). He ended the war destitute (Byers, 2005).

In my opinion labeling Schindler as an opportunist is missing the point of his existence. Schindler was a spy. Being a spy is not the work of an opportunist, though opportunity plays a part.

Even if Schindler were—as is often stated—simply a businessman who experienced a change of heart when he observed everyone in the ghetto being imprisoned and/or exterminated, acting on a change of heart requires more than opportunity. It requires commitment and courage. Perhaps Schindler, who was already a spy, initially saw Jews as cheap labor. Perhaps a small part of him even saw helping them as after-war insurance, playing both sides "just in case" Germany lost. Perhaps he saw these realities and was a wartime visionary of sorts, but seeing alone doesn't engender the courage to follow through.

The Jews were not simply his opportunity for wealth. They were also his opportunity to be executed.

From the minute Schindler helped the first Jew he was at risk for extermination himself. He was often under the microscope of Nazi examination and—during the period of his adventure into hero— was even arrested three times, with each occasion growing ever more serious.

If Schindler were simply an opportunist his history, before and after the war, would be riddled with more than a string of bankruptcies and personal failures, because for an opportunist there is always an opportunity. It is true that war presents unique circumstances, and many have succeeded within this landscape; but being in the right place at the right time is only a piece of any person's story. Recognizing the opportunity and then being moved to act requires many *Leadership Sensibility* skills.

Using behavioral thinking when reading his story as it is laid out in Wikipedia, his Leadership core appears to be the desire for Greatness, and his most accomplished sensory-driven Leadership skill, "sight," aka "looking the part."

Schindler often dressed up for the role and played out the subterfuge.

From the child who forged school documents to the husband living off rich in-laws and impregnating a mistress while driving businesses into bankruptcy, Schindler's Leadership style began long before World War II. Perhaps Schindler was a peacock trying to make a living off his plumage, but I believe he was more than that. I believe he was a Great Leader with vision that was only brought into focus by chaos. A visionary within the chaos of hate and wartime actions, Schindler had a core that risked everything including his life. He led his Jews into safety and his women into danger.

Perhaps Schindler wanted to FEEL his Greatness too much to attain it in ordinary life. Perhaps that is why—despite the learning curve of his success—once the war ended he couldn't figure out how to build richness and purpose in the day-to-day dun drum of typical business planning. Perhaps that is also why, after yet another bankruptcy, he left his wife and went back to Germany to get closer to the history of his success and to reclaim a FEELing of purpose.

But Germany was no longer at war and reclaiming his Greatness elusive. Perhaps for Schindler, life without risk, excitement, fear, and reason was a cloud of confusion. So his return to Germany resulted in even more failed businesses, and the closest he came to his own Greatness was the Jewish gratitude money that kept him alive over the years.

Schindler swung from follower to Leader many times over the course of his life. Opportunity and desire enabled him to make himself into a hero. Subterfuge and horror presented to him the urgency and vision needed for him to take all the steps necessary in order to make fantasy and desire into reality and happy endings.

However, it seems that, without danger, a resistance to typicality and self-knowledge left Schindler finding nothing real enough to fire up and unite his purpose with vision and action on a long-term basis.

Perhaps this absence of intense reality, rather than the reportedly flawed character of an opportunist, is actually what made him into a hero while also keeping him from living a long and happy life.

In a sense nothing is real.

|||||||||||||||||||||||||||||||||||||||||| ▲ ▲ ▲ |||||||||||||||||||||||||||||||||||||||||||||||

In fact **Leadership Sensibilities** is simply a phrase I am coining. It is a play on words and stems from the concept that, as mentioned, every one of your senses comes into play in the creation of your original being and, also, in the creation of the being you then become.

In fact, so powerful are your beliefs that many quantum physicists argue, on the subject of personality, that one's entire life experience is a fabrication of the mind based on a person's desires stemming from their beliefs and created by the senses. Senses which are there just to trick you into further believing you're even alive. Like a pet rock, they hypothesize that you are a brain in a box on the desk of some alien in another dimension. They also theorize your brain's deception using the model of an immersed-in-water coffin sleeper dreaming of *The Matrix* (Mo Costandi, 2006).

But brains are never, never, never, stuck in a box (though they are often in a circle) for they can imagine. And while they imagine they can incorporate sensory reality into their creation. Think about it. Your brain has the only indestructible key out of the box: IDEAS! Problem solving IDEAS! So think about it. Thinking is how you get in shape. Thinking is how you become more adept at wielding the key.

Go ahead. Think about it! It is up to you and your brain to choose what you embrace. It is up to you to decide how you will think.

> *"Reality Is An Illusion: Albeit A Very Persistent One."*
>
> ~ *Albert Einstein*

MYTH #2

Leaders have all the answers. So, though most people use less than 10% of their brain, Leaders use more.

Leaders may appear fully informed, but to be a Leader one needs only to have the "next" answer and even then only when the question arises. As for the brain, all people—Leaders included—use 100% of their brain.

If all the neurons in the brain fired at the same time, the owner of that unfortunate headpiece would die, be damaged, or at the very least have an unprecedented seizure. So obviously, in most people, the cells of their entire brain are not all firing at any one time (Bono, 2015). However, all cells of any person's brain do fire on occasion because they must; if they do not they will wither and die. And once they die, other cells will move in and take their place. These new cells, occupying the old cell's space, will fire for them. In this way—Leaders and followers—use their brain, all of it.

What *is* different is not so much the percentage of the brain that is used as the richness of the brain that is built.

The human brain runs on patterns and as such is a biological pattern making machine gathering information via sensory system networks (Weiner, 2003).

As mentioned, the brain has 100 billion neurons, even at birth. That is a huge number. To understand, know that if you sat down to count the neurons in your baby's brain, you would be counting for 95 years, an impossible task. All these billions of neurons in the human brain interact together to construct and weave strings of useful information patterns which get ever more complex as cognitive thought process increases (Schalkoff, 2011).

Since, however, function and focus change which groups of neurons are engaged and active at any given time, many people have used this "selective firing for the task at hand" as evidence that only 10% of the brain is being accessed (BlindfoldActivation, 2014). This is erroneous.

It is all used, in different configurations, at different times, for different purposes.

This is because it is through the use of varied neural patterns that the brain recognizes, organizes, stores and retrieves information when needed. Logically it is often assumed that Leaders wouldn't be Leading if they were not more complex than their followers. Thus part of the *myth* is that they are smarter and have more skill at complex reasoning.

As mentioned in the beginning of this book under "What Makes a Leader's Brain?" it has been hypothesized that the more complex the processing, the more Leader-like the brain.

However, it is sometimes the brain's limited use of cross discipline complexity and the pursuant single-mindedness of attention that breeds a Leader with the most here-to-fore unknown solutions to problems.

▼ ▼ ▼

LEADER: MARY TEMPLE GRANDIN PHD (1947–) was diagnosed with autism as a preschooler. She is known for changing an entire industry's approach to the inhumane treatment of cattle because, in some ways, she thinks like a cow. She is also known for enlightening parents and teachers on the subject of autism.

Her early life and academic career were steered by the unusual nature of her brain's processing. She was slow to speak, socially challenged, and repetitious in her behaviors and copying skills (Grandin and Panek, 2013).

It has often been postulated that autistic individuals have a perplexingly developed mirror neuron system that manifests as difficulty with requested copying contrasted by commonly adhered-to habits of echoing words and music. Dr. Grandin herself was referred to as a tape recorder and teased at school for this form of echoing.

With a desire to understand her differences from the cellular level, Temple Grandin underwent testing using modern imaging techniques. Diffusion Tensor Imaging, a method that traces connections between brain regions, made her challenged neuronal connections visible. Additionally, via magnetic resonance, an imaging technique that looks at structure, her oversized amygdala and undersized facial recognition software areas were pictured.

The unusualness in the pathways that travel from the back to the front of Dr. Grandin's brain may be part of the reason for her visual acuity. They may also be related to a misdirected mirror neuron system that should light up when a member of your species acts, or even if you just imagine that action. This "lighting up" of the circuitry is suspected of creating a sensation of familiarity and connection with your race and/or species. Due to her particular thinking process Temple Grandin responds to cattle with a sense of connection. She believes she can understand how cattle process and feel. Dr. Grandin attributes this affinity for understanding the mind of the cow, to visualization patterns caused by her autism. She has been reported to say that these skills have taught her to comprehend how changes in visual details can cause changes in sensory sensitivity in cattle (Montgomery and Grandin, 2012). This connection led her to design humane animal handling equipment that strongly influenced the way cattle are treated while being prepared for slaughter.

Despite her childhood diagnosis—or maybe because of it—Dr. Grandin's single-mindedness of visual attention to minute details led her to Lead others. Mary Temple Grandin is a highly educated award-winning speaker, prolific author, and respected scientist at the forefront of animal activism and autism education. She has brought great insight to the parents and educators of autism. She is the inventor of the Hug Box, inspired by noting that since cattle calmed in a squeeze box she might be able to calm her own anxiety in a similar fashion; she adapted the design for use with humans. Dr. Grandin is a famous Leader with autism and has stated that there is no cure; she will always be autistic.

|||||||||||||||||||||||||||||||||||||||||| ▲ ▲ ▲ ||||||||||||||||||||||||||||||||||||||||||||||

Now let me explain to you exactly how you perSEEv what you perSEEv, and what that then means about you, so that you can shape your feedback loops and purposefully change your perception in order to make the gains you wish to make in life.

Understanding how to do a thing makes desired change easier to achieve and goal accomplishment a breeze. To that end, I will tell you who you are so that you can choose (if you wish) to be different, quieter, louder, tougher, softer, more empathetic, more enigmatic, whatever suits your goals and wishes.

Let me Lead you with information so that you can Lead yourself and others with love and strength.

> **"As You Think, So Shall You Be."**
>
> *Wayne W. Dyer*

MYTH #3

Leaders don't work hard; they work smart, because they are smart. Leaders' "smarts" are in their head.

Actually Leaders' "smarts" are in their behavior, even the behavior in their head. "Smarts" are also in the body, in the gut, and in the heart, it's said.

To the second point: In fact Leaders work very hard; they are the first to start (usually with the idea) and the last to quit (because they define the length of the project). So though Leaders often work smarter than others, they also work more. In fact, most Leaders prefer work to play because work is their play. They love to engage, accomplish, create, and overcome (Wiseman and McKeown, 2010).

To do this humans have been equipped with multiple body brains and sophisticated nervous systems all communicating together within their bodies.

True Leaders use all of the intelligence available to them. They go far beyond the use of just their head brain. An effective Leader does work smarter by using all of three different body brains: gut, heart, and skull in unison and balance. This concept gives a whole new meaning to phrases such as "gut instinct" and being "true to your heart." So, Leaders need to use not only their heads, but also the innate intelligence and wisdom of their whole body as it communicates and informs them via the Seven Senses of Leadership.

Fortunately, tapping into your Leadership Senses can be learned, and the solution is largely in giving attention from the brain to the behavior of the body. For example, if you are tense in a meeting, check your breathing. If it is fast and shallow, slow it down while breathing with your tummy. Know the tricks of immediate self-change: your posture informs your mood as does your facial expression. You cannot feel sad while smiling with face and eyes, and standing erect reduces negative ideation. In fact, when you use power poses, like sitting upright with legs and arms open, your cortisol goes down, your testosterone goes up, and you become more fully integrated with all of your brains.

Stand strong, think strong.

In the increasingly complex and volatile social/business environments in which organizations operate, Leaders who are unable to connect with and harness the intrinsic intelligence of those multiple head, heart, and gut brains are at a distinct disadvantage.

Yes, Leaders work smarter but they also work harder, from head to toe.

In fact, sometimes "stick-to-it-iveness" and "working harder" is what creates their Leadership position in the first place.

LEADER: DANIEL RUETTIGER (1948-), more commonly known as "RUDY," was supposed to speak in a James Malinchak Big Money Speaker seminar I attended. Unfortunately he was very sick and barely made it to his hotel room at the conference, let alone onto the stage. RUDY is the real-life character made famous in the film RUDY. Thus the film story is the one most known: RUDY who was the third child in a family of sixteen, had a dream to play football for Notre Dame, and did (Ruettiger, 2012).

RUDY was dyslexic and his grades were too low for Notre Dame. But, after many side routes and four application attempts, his hard work, persistence, definition of purpose, and the absolute belief that he could make it happen paid off. RUDY managed to get accepted to the University. However, getting onto the football team required even more steadfast hard work and persistence. RUDY had many hurdles. For example, to name just a few, he was small—5'6" and 165 lbs— and he had a lack of natural skill. Despite the impediments RUDY managed to be placed on the practice team. His absolute passion and fortitude were so admirable that eventually—on the last game of his senior year—RUDY was dressed and asked to get on the field.

Despite RUDY's lack of scored points or importance to the actual plays of the game itself, RUDY was an inspiration to the players and became one of only two Notre Dame players ever to be carried from the field (Ruettiger, 2012).

RUDY, both the movie and the man, were unstoppable motivating forces.

The movie spread inspiration internationally, and RUDY reached into the hearts and minds of a generation of up-and-coming athletes Leading them to dig deep and "work harder" eventually culminating in the High School Football "Rudy" Awards in search of being recipients that personify the "Four C's of Courage, Character, Commitment, and Contribution."

Rudy's journey to get the film made personifies all Four of those C's and was equally as challenging as the journey of acceptance into Notre Dame. Rudy shopped this movie idea all over Hollywood as "a nobody." Getting it made was against all odds. But he did it. I began this Leader story by telling you that I was supposed to see Rudy speak at a conference but that he was sick. And that is true. However, now I am revealing something else. He spoke anyway.

That is how I know so much about his story. He told it from the stage of that conference between waves of full body sweats, nausea and discomfort.

He was inspiring us and creating empathy even as a man with most of his career behind him.

When you represent yourself honestly in the world, you are always a living example of your message. So get to know yourself and your Senses, your motivators, and Leadership Sensibilities, so that you can be true to you.

Match your message...

...like RUDY, the man on the stage, showing us a real-life example of the type of man it takes to Lead and inspire others to work hard with a purpose in mind.

|||||||||||||||||||||||||||||||||||||||||||||| ▲ ▲ ▲ ||||||||||||||||||||||||||||||||||||||||||||||||

About the senses of perSEption:

Since I opened the concept of perSEption with an example of perSEEving, let's begin with **SIGHT.**

> *"We are what we repeatedly do. Excellence, then, is not an act but a habit."*
>
> *~ Will Durant (not Aristotle to whom this quote is often attributed)*

Chapter One

SENSE ONE in the SEVEN SENSES of LEADERSHIP

MYTH #4

Leaders who are leading are obviously not broken and need no help to keep their eyes on the sights of success.

A Leader's vision comes from within. But their assessment of success and the ability to remain an outward awareness of their follower's needs and desires requires a network of supports.

Leaders are able to SEE the value of what is offered them as they shop in the world of peak performance aids. Leaders are always looking to peak their performance.

This is because Leaders SEE success in the smallest of adjustments.

Just as the Olympic athlete works tirelessly to shave a fraction of a second off their time so, too, does any Leader reach for new and improved results despite *the law of diminishing returns*. All Leaders envision and SEE the very real truth that little differences gather together to make big differences. All Leaders are willing to do the work required to make those differences come to fruition. And though all Leaders may not appear to be Olympic athletes, in this visionary way they are all similar; they just play in different playgrounds.

Leaders commit to peak performance training. They are committed to improvement, and as such they have usually amassed enough knowledge and experience to SEE a lot of value in just one new idea, one mental or physical enhancement, one connection never before made.

Neurofeedback is a brainwave driven computer game. It teaches the brain how to correct and adjust at each step in the creation of itself, each step that is related to a particular brain state in order to enhance whatever skill is being engaged in by each individual (Evans, 2007). Many high-powered businesspeople, athletes, artists, and metaphysical Leaders use neurofeedback to disengage from the tunnel vision of stress and become more focused, congruent in all three of their "knowing centers:" heart, gut, and brain (Friis, Seaward, and Dayer-Berenson, 2013).

Leaders SEEk the skill of eliminating distractions and removing fear from high-pressure situations. So a therapy that teaches the brain to improve itself and attain a visionary Zen state at will is of great value. Neurofeedback does just that. It requires no skill or IQ to use. It simply shows the brain waves to the "player" by representing them as a game. The brain naturally shifts focus in order to play. Anyone can do it, but the Leader's Leadership inclinations help them play to win by focusing on the goal. And then they get what they are SEEking, that desired Zen state.

Focusing the brain eliminates stress and anxiety, and Leaders are fully aware of the exponential benefits of constant cognitive control. There are many different ways to exercise and focus the brain, some less precise or potent than others, but all of value. In my experience neurofeedback is king, but a simple crossword puzzle, Sudoku, online brain games like Luminosity, IQ tests in Mensa booklets, MindWare games like Qwirkle, spatial games with 3D puzzles, memory-based card games, etc. are all of value. With every one of these pastimes you have the opportunity to exercise and gain intellectual focus benefits, as long as you are not already superior at that particular game.

In fact, gaining skills can even be done the old-fashioned way; for example, in the car surrounded by rambunctious, technology deprived children in need of entertaining. Word games, math games, and memory games can all be made up and are great for bonding and brain health, because, yes, even Leaders have to SEE to their children.

Factors related to wellbeing (such as hours slept a night) and the beauty of one's environment can change anxiety markedly. Performance is linked to psychological wellbeing. And psychological wellbeing is linked to performance. Everything is linked to health habits (Friis et al., 2013).

Proper sleep, balanced diet, reduced stress, and regular exercise are just some of the things that can contribute to improved cognitive performance and brain health (Fahey, Insel, and Roth, 2007).

Fortunately, even if you have abused your brain with drugs or poor habits, most brain damage can be reversed (Carson, 2012), (Amen, 2009).

One easily accessible example of how to effect a healing even in late adulthood is steady aerobic exercise of over 30 minutes four times a week to release brain neurotrophic factors (Corradi, 2013) and create higher gray matter volume. Exercise is even more beneficial done in nature as the fresh air and beauty enhance mood and enjoyment as well as provide a sense of perspective and awe.

In addition, more and more science is proving that food can, and does, have profound effects on the brain. This is obvious if you think about it. Your car only runs on the fuel intended for it, and even then it needs to be clean. The human challenge is not being placated into self-abuse by the fact that our magnificent bodies can compensate, counteract, and create new pathways to try and cope with the assault we give them.

With care, your brain and body will be able to do that for a very long time.

However, as people age their system breaks down, they absorb nutrients differently, their vision diminishes, and individualized routines of vitamin supplements become a near necessity (Mann and Truswell, 2012).

Leaders have architecturally different brains from followers, so you cannot apply typical rules and analogies of advice like "slow down and smell the roses" to understand or improve how Leaders function. Leaders' brains are sharpest when they are doing the deciding, so they like to decide things in order to become Zen. However, when Leaders have been dosing themselves with adrenalin and cortisol in order to focus in states of tension and stress, they may become focused but they will not become Zen-like and will break down faster. Leaders, fortunately and unfortunately, are often a challenge to teach. They frequently drop out of school because they have enough vision to SEE what is required to proceed. And they often overwork themselves because they can SEE what it takes to succeed.

So if you want to Lead, learn how to not get into a self-destructive anxiety loop now. Make different choices, catch your damaging habits, and reverse the damage as the damage is done.

The beauty of your brain is that, like getting Lasik surgery for your eyes, your vision can be renewed to a state of youthful acuity, again and again and again (Hicks, 2014).

SENSE ONE

SEEING

The physiology of seeing is really complex. SEEing is not simply done with the eyes. I remember learning about sight in grade school. It was all very logical and easily explained, like understanding the camera, magical yet explainable. Back then they taught that light comes in through the pupil, and goes to the back of the head where there's this little screen that the light projects its image on, like a movie projector and screen. The way they explained vision, it seemed as if people must have heads as empty of shadow-creating obstacles as the air above the moviegoers hoping to enjoy a picture show. But, in fact, empty headedness and this version of vision are like urban myths. They hold a flicker of fact for credibility, but upon closer inspection turn out to be completely false! So much more goes into seeing than an empty head.

We could break sight down to the cones in the eye itself, which ones read color and which ones don't read color. We could add how the frequencies of the vibrations in the light are figured out. Or we could follow the light down the optic nerve pathway. We could watch half of the information from each eye go one direction in the brain, and the other half of the information from each eye go a different direction (Brownedu, 2000).

A lot of people believe that they see on the right with their right eye, and on the left with their left eye. Well, in fact, that's another flicker-of-truth myth that is mostly incorrect. You actually see on the right utilizing the visual field from the *right half* of your right eye and the *right half* of your left eye, and you see on the left by utilizing the *left half* of your left eye and the *left half* of your right eye (Rybolt and Rybolt, 2009). Half of everything sort of crosses over and merges with its partnering half before traveling back, through the brain, to the back of the head where, in fact, *now* we would use the analogy of a sort of projector screen. It is here that the picture is put together or fully compiled out of that first divided, then partly merged, information. The picture is put together at the back of the brain. It's called the occipital lobe (Singh, 2008). It's at the very back. How ridiculous is that?

There must be some evolutionary reason to have things be so complex and hence so open to error. Obviously the more actions there are to take and the longer the path to travel, the more opportunities for collapse. In the case of sight, visual information comes in, breaks apart, travels the full distance of the brain, and then recompiles while getting decoded, and that's the simplified explanation (Zhaoping and Li, 2014).

By this point in our evolution we all understand that no two computers are exactly alike. They all have quirks. Our brains are even more open to interpretive error or difference than a computer is because they are organic and evolving in response to the environment. Thus, each individual brain is likely to decode this vibrational information slightly differently; differently from other brains and differently from itself at the different stages and ages of its existence (Braverman, 2013). Since that is true the question is, *"Why? Why would nature set us up to be so full of places on the road wherein difference can be magnified?"*

Perhaps this complexity is the visual version of the Bible's *Tower of Babble.* **Perhaps we are meant to be isolated from each other, unable to correctly communicate what we See because what others say they See is denied by our version of what we experience Seeing?** Perhaps difference is the point? And since difference being inevitable is undeniably true, then you better understand uniqueness or you won't be able to Lead anyone other than yourself, because you will be the only one with your version of perSEEing.

Many people find all this too loosely structured, and thus too overwhelming. So, in need of clearer answers, they create methods and dictates intended to force everyone into a pattern of sameness.

Forcing compliance by refusing difference and insisting on shaping everyone into becoming one big assembly line of cloned humanity is not Leading; it's lying. It's the kind of lying you can find in the army, the church, the educational system, or at the airport.

Behave like a wolf and the sheep will feed you. Till they die. But they will die. And though you may go down in history as a Leader you won't have Led; you will have eaten sheep.

If you want to Lead you must first be so completely self-aware that you emit the light of your truth just by being! Thus, your people will follow the light and find you. Nobody can be a Leader to all, though some are seen by almost all as formidable, insightful, ingenious, etc. The important part to becoming a beacon of motivation is to see clearly, see yourself first, your goals, motivations, and intentions (James Clear, 2016).

This is a must because a murky picture doesn't glow very bright, and as such it's hard for your potential followers to follow out of their confusion. So learn how to be a clear, bright, *unmissable* picture, by gathering yourself into a strong awareness of you, and the path you are leading them down.

See to be Seen has a new twist when considered in this light.

Your vision is your beginning. And if you understand how you see, you can correct for any anomalies or errors in judgment. So read this over and over until you perSEEv and thoroughly comprehend the Leader's sense of Sight, because understanding is the key to intentional success.

Now for a little more vision science. Yes, science is also a belief.

As if all that visual complexity weren't mindboggling enough.

I didn't even give you the full information. There's so much more.

For example, there are different streams of optical information that have little to do with the right and left field of vision. Some streams will tell you when you see motion, and some of them will tell you when you see stillness. Thus, it is possible to be blind to motion but not inanimate objects and vice versa. What a freaky world that would be! And what an interesting analogy for how some people only see Leaders when they are on the move while others see those who stand their ground and stay in place. Fact is—Leader or follower—everything we do on the inside is reflected in how we behave on the outside. This is another reason to understand that difference has nothing to do with accuracy or rightness and everything to do with being yourself and letting your people find you. There are plenty of people to help; you don't need every one of them, and every one of them doesn't need you. Additionally, you don't need any of them, and none of them need you, forever.

You may discount these bits and pieces of information because I am using extreme examples like blindness to motion. However, extreme examples are often used to help people understand the more subtle struggles of their day-to-day existence.

So yes, it is true that most people's issues with these visual information streams are more likely to be subtle than total, as in motion blindness. In some ways, though, subtle is worse because it is less obvious and more convincingly confusing. For example, distortions in motion—distortions that you believe everyone is seeing—(think of your friend with the extreme startle reflex) can make you seem timid and scared while distortions in stillness (the cup that you just set down doesn't seem to be there anymore even though it's right under your nose) can make you appear stupid or forgetful.

These "differences" are likely to be distortions that are never detected because everyone has some variation with these things, so there is a type of social sharing, myth creation, and support for the problems they create.

Additionally, if you see it that way, for you that is the way it is seen by everyone. It's just not obvious enough as a difference from others to be detected rather than accepted. In fact, acceptance of our differences is something we do in this altered reality way all the time. However, acceptance isn't always the end result. Perceptual challenges are often whittled down to *my* truth versus *your* truth and can be the source of conflict: Ask any husband and wife that ever fought about color. (Heterosexual men perSEEv fewer colors on the light spectrum than many women and homosexual men do. So ladies, if the two of you are not fighting about color maybe you should check his Saturday night poker game group for crushes and gay lovers. LOL).

Even, and maybe especially, in marriage it would be better if we accepted all differences with purposeful intention.

In Leadership I SEE that as your job: Lead and accept.

Then Lead to accept.

That is why I'm trying to get across the physiology of Seeing. To help you understand that perSEEving anything visually is hugely affected by all of these different moments in the path of creating. This puzzle that is decoded from frequencies of light coming in your eye and then recreated as a picture is easily distorted and individualized. In fact, you put the picture together at the back of the head upside down, and then you have to perSEEv it right side up. What if *your* brain doesn't know how to do that? What would you perSEEv?

I mean, there's just so much that goes on, and at any point in that pathway it can be broken. So, when it breaks, you now perSEEv differently from the masses. Sometimes that difference is what makes you a Leader.

In fact, brain different is what Leaders are.

If you are following this thinking you may be brain different enough to Lead.

Perhaps you have what it takes to perSEEv that there are so many places in this pathway where SEEing can be bent enough to change the picture, that it also changes the person's perception and resultant life purpose.

You can be bent into something great. You can be bent and not broken. I believe they call that "out of the box." Different: From eyesight to execution.

Yes, you can be bent and then, as you try to use your version of reality to move forward in life, your version of reality is going to be influenced by experience and adjust itself, refining those bends and twists, over and over again.

Creating a unique and individualized you. A Leader. Or not. Depending upon your motives, intentions, problems, and ideas.

For example, if one person's right side of the right eye operates a little differently than another person's, then they're going to see *slightly* differently. And if those streams of visual information are passed at a different rate, they're going to see differently in a maladaptive way. Some people see wiggly things. Some people see hallucinations. Some people see sound and some see energy. There are just so many places where your vision can be affected, that it can't be one hundred percent trusted and then compared to someone else's as evidence of truth. Thus eyewitness testimony is excruciatingly unreliable.

And every one of us SEES according to our physical capabilities and then justifies that reality with psychological adaptations.

And every one of us SEES according to the physical reconstruction in our brains that was undergone via those same psychological adaptations.

Beliefs are our builder's tools. And we are always at work.

Do you SEE it now? I bet you do!

But, wait! There's more!

So far, we've just been talking about the hardware of the physiology of Seeing, but there's even an operating system to the physiology of Seeing before we get into the psychological aspects, which we could call the software. I am comparing to a computer model or some other sophisticated bit of equipment to help you See that you're always going to have these different components, places where things can break down.

But I could as easily use the metaphor of a car. If we were looking at a car we'd have the computer in the car, we'd have the fuel for the car, and we'd have the structure of the car (Eddie Harmon-Jones, 2009). Almost everything man has made to perform a function could be referenced as an example.

So, let's use that metaphor. The car is the hardware like the eyes and the brain matter. The operating system is the cellular instructions in the DNA and protein synthesis, and the fuel is the neurochemistry. The neurochemistry of your brain changes how and what you See just as the quality and availability of the fuel in a car defines how well it runs. In the brain, if you have a whole lot of serotonin flooding the system, you see differently than if you have a whole lot of dopamine or cortisol. With each new neurochemical bath you see differently (Arden, 2010), (Arden, 2012). This is in part because each of these will create a different sort of focus of attention.

Just to be quick and easy about it, consider dopamine as a motivating hormone. It would probably bring you to notice things in your environment that are more likely to motivate you into action, you will see with a finely tuned focus (Rubin and Pfaff, 2010). The details would get really sharp and the distractions reduced from your awareness, and this would help to give you lots of energy for the things you want to accomplish. You'd be in the hyper-focused zone, talking fast, laughing quickly, taking immediate action on the things your "fuel" had helped you see. That's why cocaine has a similar effect on you—because it makes it so that you have more access to your dopamine (Jr, R.P.H., 1995).

Conversely, if you have a lot of serotonin flooding your system (again, this is really simplified), you might feel a little bit more "chill," and then the things that come into your attention change into items that encourage relaxation and calm (Hart, 2008). When the things that come into your attention change because your mood changed, because your desire to take action changed, *then you SEE differently.*

We have all noticed some version of this phenomenon. For example, you're about to buy a gold car, and you never really noticed gold cars before; but on your way to find the gold car that you found on Craigslist, you see gold cars everywhere. So, gold car, after gold car, after gold car, your vision is being chosen by your experience because now your mind is seeing the thing that's been brought to its attention. Depending upon how you've been affected by your neurochemistry, different things will come to your attention (Perry, Ashton, and Young, 2002). For example, if you were nervously shooting the stress hormone cortisol into your system while looking for the gold car you may see *no* gold cars. Or you may see nothing *but* gold cars, depending upon the beliefs surrounding your stress because that's what your brain does: It gives you substantiate evidence about your worries and joys as it decodes your experiences.

We could talk about SEEing for days and days and just get the tip of the iceberg. But the important, re-shapeable part to understand is in this example: If it was a fear-based neurochemical release, you'd look for things that were dangerous, and you'd find them! Because, what you look for, you find. What you SEEk, you find. Absolutely. Even if you were tucked safely in bed, you'd find a sharp edge to worry about banging your head on or a noise to hide from. If you feel like you are in danger you have to find the source of the danger.

Your neurochemistry affects you very much, and how you end up with that bath of neurochemistry is largely related to how your physiology combines with your psychology (McGuigan, 1987).

IIIIIIIIIIIIIIIIIIIIIIIIIIIIIIIIIIIIIIIIIIII ▼ ▼ ▼ IIIIIIIIIIIIIIIIIIIIIIIIIIIIIIIIIIIIIIIIIIIIIIIII

LEADER: HELEN ADAMS KELLER (1880–1968) and Johanna Anne Mansfield Sullivan Macy (1866–1936) had lives of inspiration that brought vision to all, even the visually impaired. Both women lost their sight as children due to illness. Helen Keller, however, was younger, more of an infant at the time, and lost her hearing as well. When Helen was six years old and Anne was twenty the two met, and by Leading each other through the darkness of social ambiguity they Learned to Learn from each other. This changed the beliefs about and possibilities for blind and deaf people around the world. Their story is so profound and Helen— once she could express herself—became so proactive, that their tale has been made into a movie many times over (Seka, 2014).

Their Story (in all likelihood and according to today's science): Helen was nearly without communication when Anne, whose sight had been marginally restored via surgery, arrived to teach Helen sign language. Anne's ability to teach and reach the non-communicative Helen was challenged by many things, most notably the fact that Helen didn't even comprehend the concept that every object had a name. After many struggles and with great persistence, Anne managed to enlighten Helen and bring a vision of things into her mind via language. She did this by touching the object and then performing signs on Helen's hand (Keller, 1985). After that Helen was a voracious learner who eventually managed speech. She traveled globally speaking, winning awards, writing articles, writing books, and being a friend to powerful people.

SEEing for Helen—like for everyone—was something that happened in the mind. But for Helen it happened without the decoding of information about the vibrations of light reaching her occipital cortex. SIGHT for Helen came from the ability to perSEEv the concept of things via touch.

Regardless of how the images were formed, they were accompanied by the chemical bath of SEEing; vibration decoding pathways and networks formed anyway. The network of hearing and SEEing through physical connection created words and sounds via vibration touch sensors in the fingertips. And if we had the imaging techniques then that we have now, we would likely find a huge representation of these rerouted phenomena in the sensory cortex. This is the magic of compensatory mechanisms in the brain. We can build ourselves, and we do, according to our actions and beliefs (Kissin, 2012).

This sensory network is only the inner network of the brain and body; the miracle of Helen required much more than that. She needed an outer network as well. She needed to dance the Leader dance of teacher student/ student teacher and was fortunate enough to have Anne as a willing partner. When Helen was unaware of object naming, no conceptual understanding of her world could be formed and passed to others in order to be built upon and passed back again. Anne had begun the teaching with pre-decided lists of signed words but quickly noticed that Helen was not responding to these. She adapted her style and switched to words based upon Helen's interests. This new understanding added to Anne's vision of her blind/deaf student who blossomed before her from challenged student to brilliant girl. Once Anne got the idea of objects having names across to Helen, Helen's mind's eye began to form concepts into things. This gave Helen communicative SIGHT. As Anne watched Helen grow in sophistication she likely grew as well.

These inner and outer workings are some of the components that must have compiled Helen's network of SIGHT. It is in the passing of a belief, an understanding, a concept, from Anne to Helen and from

Helen to Anne, that SIGHT is given to both. Swimming in ambiguity is formless, but with identification things take shape and become SEEable. Emotions, like the fear of being controlled, by unSEEable hands moving her about likely blocked and diminished her ability to SEE through imagination. However, the liberation and joy of having her own outer world decoder would have made identification, connection, and networking visible. And that supported SIGHT can reshape and propel a willingness to learn.

So like all people, sighted and not, for Helen SEEing happened from within and without because of a network that functioned for a common goal. And like all people, regardless of if there are or aren't light vibrations reaching the cortex, SEEing is colored by emotions.

IIIIIIIIIIIIIIIIIIIIIIIIIIIIIIIIIIIIIIIIIIIIIII ▼   ▼   ▼ IIIIIIIIIIIIIIIIIIIIIIIIIIIIIIIIIIIIIIIIIIIIIIIIIII

So, now let's focus in on beliefs and the perSEption of all SIGHT.

We sort of started there already, with the belief of being in danger, so let's go with that.

Let's imagine you grew up as a child with the idea that if you were locked in a room you might burn to death in a fire. And all of a sudden your door breaks, and you can't get out; and this belief from when you were young really pounds into you. You don't even know why you're feeling so panicked yet you are panicking. You start pulling on that door frantically.

Now cortisol is flooding your system, adrenaline is flooding your system, and you are looking for either a way out or looking for what's going to hurt you; and depending on which you are looking for you will find different answers; you will *See differently*. Things that are harmless will become dangerous, things that are not sharp will become sharp, and things that are not hot will look like they are about to burst into flame. You will See a different world than whoever else opens the door, walks in, and says, "What are you talking about? It's perfectly fine in here."

So, what you believe changes what you See. It also changes what you have the ability to See—and this is the piece that's often left out—how your brain is able to process those light waves that come into your eye. How your brain is able to process them and how your eye is able to deal with them, *the whole mechanism*, also changes what you SEE and what is seen. Your ability to perSEEv is changed by your SEEing habits: the bits and pieces of what you have thus far seen.

If you want to be in control of the way that you see the world, this is good news because you can do one of two things: You can change your physiology, or you can change your psychology. Both are possible and either one will change the other.

Most people think they can only change their experience by changing their psychology. But putting on a pair of glasses or sunglasses doesn't simply affect your physiology (Friedman and Hartelius, 2015). It also changes your experience of what you See, which changes what you know to be true and then changes your beliefs and psychological outlook.

Now, let's apply this to Leadership. If I want to be a Leader, or I am a Leader but I want to be better at it, I need to make sure that I'm like the horse that's running a race. I have my blinders on and am fully focused on the goal of reaching the finish line.

I have to work in concert with my jockey and tune up my awareness of the other horses running the race so that I don't bump into them. Thus, I can't be completely blind. Awareness of others and working in concert with your partner is the part that people often forget when using this analogy.

> *"Some men see things as they are and say why. I dream things that never were and say why not."*
>
> ~ George Bernard Shaw

Keep your awareness of others.

Even as you motivate yourself, delete the distractions and focus straight down the tunnel at your goal.

Don't be delusional about your motives.

Being myopic does not mean you are using motivated neurochemistry to focus. An experience alone is not enough to tell you about yourself. Some people get their tunnel vision from deadlines and pressure (Jay, 2009). Therefore, they think pressure is good. But they also get their heart attacks and nervous breakdowns from the same habits.

Understand: everything that is good can look bad and vice versa. As my neuropsychology professor used to say, "The devil's in the details."

So, motivation and stress both cause tunnel vision (Szalma and Hancock, 2012). And this is a quandary for people who are trying to become better Leaders and purposefully stress themselves. They bathe their system in constant cortisol in order to have that single-mindedness-of-purpose and tunnel their vision to focus at the goal.

Unfortunately, what they lose while doing it this way is an awareness of the other horses—the ability to take good care of their people. So, don't do it that way. Believing that stress, panic, and last-minute pressure is making you better is actually making you worse (Weisinger and Pawliw-Fry, 2015). This is true despite the evidence you perSEEv to the contrary. This habit is accompanied by a supporting belief which is making you see your success differently, perSEEv your environment incorrectly.

One way to hack into that feedback loop in order to change it is to change the reinforcing belief. This is a psychological approach that will also shift your physiology and the cycle will change. I'm going to use this belief as the example, but we could use many. Now, let's say that you're trying to be a Leader, but your teams keep having mutinies against you. This is a clue that perhaps you're not carefully considering the needs of your people because you don't perSEEv them as important.

You don't perSEEv them as important because you actually don't see them. They're not in your awareness.

What you want to do is just change that belief: The one about them not being important.

If you change that belief, the one telling you that stress is good, panic or pressure makes you better or more efficient, you will change how you operate. You will change what you See. You will change your entire vision of the world and of what success might be. That's one of the ways to break into the loop and correct a vision problem.

You could also have done this by shifting the physiology of your brain or your eyes by using, for example, something like neurofeedback and increasing the dopamine in the left frontal lobe, which would have encouraged you to perSEEv and befriend others (Selby, 2003).

Okay now, let's imagine you have a physiological vision problem, and let's say you have an issue with seeing certain colors. Let's pretend that you don't See red and you know it's a problem when you go to the stoplights, so you've memorized where the red is on the stoplight. In the places where you know red is important, you've put it in. You have an awareness and a knowledge of red, but you still don't See red. You can do the same thing for other places where red is not so much necessary as desirable, but first you have to open up your mind to understand that it's not just important to See red at the stoplight, or when someone's face turns red with anger, but that you want to See the red everywhere in the world.

You want to be aware of the fact that you CAN put invisible things into your awareness, through belief.

Believing you can do it makes it so that you do it. Since the brain can't discern fact from fiction, if you believe you See it then you do. The irony here is that sometimes just such an approach works to remove this aspect of color blindness. Red is a hot temperature kind of emotion, and so if you want to See the color in a person's emotion, if you want to See not just Feel the heat of burning metal, then perSEEv it and re-teach your brain how to decode whatever evidence it can perSEEv via whatever frequencies it is able to recognize.

An awareness will bring red into your world, even if your red looks different from someone else's. So, again, you're breaking into the physiology with a belief, or an awareness, or an intention.

This is good news. This means that when you understand how you perSEEv, there's always a way into the loop, to break the pattern that you may have found yourself in, and correct your problem—regardless of whether it's physiology or psychology.

If you're physically blind we're going to have to use different senses to perSEEv with, but regardless of these physical limitations, you will still SEE whatever you are able to perSEEv.

And that is what is meant by the phrase, "In my mind's eye!"

Chapter Two

SENSE TWO in the SEVEN SENSES of LEADERSHIP

MYTH #5

All leaders are Type A left-brained
personalities.

A Type A Leader might be defined as a testy character with excessive drive, ambition, competitiveness, impatience, focus on quantity over quality, and a need for control.

This is not a Leader; it's a grouchy control freak with hemorrhoids!

All jokes aside, embracing a definition like this as having anything to do with Leadership sets people up to enter into, and allow to happen, Leader-follower relationships of abuse. When medical science categorizes a behavioral type, somehow it becomes acceptable. Labeling a boss as Type A is generally followed by a shrug and a sigh of acquiescence, as if there is nothing a person can do. This is incorrect. Leave.

If followers stay with these Fake Leaders they end up feeling responsible for that Leader's emotional state. Instead of the Leader having a Type A coronary, it is probable that the follower will.

Don't be that person—either of them.

An interesting bit of brain science that belies the Left Brain Leader concept is found during moments of inspiration. An epiphany appears to cause 40HZ oscillations over the right temporal lobe (Kumari, Bob, and Boutros, 2014). Most Leaders are great "idea" people having "aha" moments or epiphanies on a regular basis. So, despite the fact that "rational" thought (defined as logical and analytical) does originate more from regions of the left brain, Leaders need the right brain to fully function. Creativity, conceptual speech, sensory integration, putting the picture together, and comprehending time as well as space requires the right, temporal lobe, parietal lobe, and cingulate gyrus plus more (Kemmerer, 2014).

Arbitrarily dividing the brain into right and left and then labeling people one or the other is misLeading. Leaders are not nasty people who can't interact any better than an empowered two-year-old having a temper tantrum.

Why would you want to follow that? And if nobody is following what qualifies this person as a Leader?

Today's business no longer thrives as well in a top-down model. Followers and Leaders are too connected both socially and in business matters around the world. Thus any Leader with such a segregated concept will wither, not thrive. Emotional intelligence and intuition are as much a Leadership skill as marketing and financial planning are (Porter-O'Grady and Malloch, 2010). And in today's market Leaders serve their followers, making the Leader the follower and the follower the Leader, who follows.

Mindfulness, vulnerability, transparency, sharing, and serving are the new hallmarks of a Leader (L. Carter, Ulrich, and Goldsmith, 2012). A Leader uses it all—the right, the left, the front, the back, the brain, the body, the inside, the outside, all interconnected—passing knowledge and information through the Senses thereby serving to grow a person into someone rich with insight and positive intention.

Passion and energy are born of this.

SENSE TWO

HEARING

The Here in Hearing Sound is indescribably important! Without it our awareness of the present moment can be extremely challenged. Sound brings you to, or away from, the Here and now. It can force external focus or internal processing upon you, dependent upon its tone and/or informational content. You probably never thought of sound in this way. But maybe you should. Fact is, you can't harness what you don't understand, and sound is a tool full of trickery unless you understand it.

So let me introduce you to the HERE in HEARING!

Of course, everything that I previously mentioned about vision also applies to sound. As with decoding Sight, decoding Sound requires many neuronal processing pathways along which, at any time, any puny little particle can break down and wreak havoc (Baars and Gage, 2010). Point in fact: a tiny floating protein can throw you into a state of vertigo that sets you to vomiting and makes reality spin while time stands still (Media, 2012). And though Sound doesn't construct itself onto a projector screen in the back of the brain like vision does, it does travel along parallel pathways (Pickles, 2012). Hearing even adds to the art of perSEEving by intersecting with SEEing at a certain juncture in the brain and then leaving a footprint. As you will learn, what you Hear collaborates with what you See to create your Here and now.

And sometimes what you Hear is weird.

Sometimes things break down and sometimes it happens Here, at the juncture between SEEing and HEARing.

This sensory junction is called the angular gyrus and it is the location wherein a confusion of senses (like seeing, hearing, tasting, number, and shape recognition) can occur (Gazzaniga, 2004). When things run amuck information can accidently travel along the wrong path. When this happens one can find themselves HEARing music if they see colors and/or SEEing color if they Hear music. In fact, the issue is bigger than this. The collision of sensory pathways can be more profound than simply setting a snag in the processing of Sight and Sound.

It can be an absolute catastrophe, like a perpetual LSD trip comprised of a kaleidoscope of unpredictable sensations. It can be an all-encompassing experience or simply just a difference, like being the person who Tastes shapes and is emotionally tormented by numbers.

And, though there are other physiological reasons for this type of sensory phenomena, junction confusion (Dere, 2012) is a good one to consider because it analogizes many Leaders and their attention confusion in business, purpose, and bright ideas. Being able to choose and then filter so we can focus is the secret to success in almost all things. But that's not what I am here to talk about, yet.

For now, we are Here to talk about HEREing!

To help you understand how Hearing helps your HEREing, let's consider a well-known, yet fairly simple syndrome: Tinnitus.

For those of you that don't know, tinnitus is the existence of a mostly constant sound in the head. Many people think of it as ringing in the ears (Henry and Wilson, 2002), (Hallam, 1989). However, tinnitus comes in other forms as well, like the sound of an ocean or the whistling of the wind or even a heartbeat echoing between your ears. (I am tempted to point out at this juncture that the head is where emotions are felt, so perhaps having a heart beating in the head is the most accurate form of tinnitus to suffer from, but that would be a digression so I won't.) (Møller, Langguth, DeRidder, and Kleinjung, 2010)

There are a lot of people who believe that tinnitus is caused by cilia—little hairs in the inner ear that regulate sound waves—incorrectly wiggling and creating a neuron signal that shouldn't be happening (Cowen, 2015). The belief is that this signal is stuck in the *on* position and consistently decoding a sound that isn't there. This makes sense since to change vibrations into tones, a cluster of neurons has to phase-lock and send the decoded signal to your conscious awareness (Haken, 2007), (Domany, 1996). Perhaps the phase-lock, locks.

However, more recently, there's a lot of evidence suggesting that tinnitus happens in many places in the head. I agree with this theory because I use neurofeedback to change brain function and have seen many brain areas respond to brain change by increasing, relieving, or creating tinnitus (Moller, Langguth, Hajak, Kleinjung, and Cacace, 2007).

Perhaps when different brain areas change how and when they decode information, pathways—previously considered unrelated to Sound processing—become broken and affect your filtering devices, your ability to pay attention—again, just like vision— to the parts you're supposed to pay attention to so you no longer accurately block out the rest.

After all, your brain is firing neurons. In all likelihood it's a noisy place since it's full of lightning storms and cascading hormones. Perhaps we are not imagining non-existent noise so much as not filtering or focusing out the sounds we were not meant to Hear within our head.

When you think about the ability to focus filter and control any of your senses, it's easy to see how their efficiency would affect your Here and now, your awareness of the present moment. But if your eyes are doing funny things, you can close your lids. It's a little harder to close your ears; harder, but not impossible.

So why do I say that HEARing is so much more impactful on you're Here and now than your other senses? Because it is a component of how HEARing works.

Sound can grab your attention or lull you into complacency.

In order to control which of these is happening to you, it is important to be able to purposely Hear the person in the foreground and not have the sounds in the background interfere, unless they are signaling danger for you or a loved one. Unfortunately, this sensory skill is often broken down by our noise pollution world. When it breaks down—as I mentioned—one of the things you may Hear are the sounds occurring inside your head.

Imagine that your head is this huge, universal storm firing neurons all over the place. Obviously, it's noisy. This must be true even if there are insulating spaces creating the eerie quiet of outer space, because each active brain cell would be loud like the birth of earth or a collapsing star. For the brain that can suddenly Hear all of this cacophony, the noise would be deafening. It would be like listening to your gut digest. We—our brains and bodies—are always under construction and construction is noisy. Therefore, we have to be able to filter out sound from both the outside and the inside.

And, as mentioned, sometimes that ability to filter and/or focus is broken.

And that causes misinformation in your Here and now.

How does sound help you with your HEREing?

Or rather, how does HEARing turn into HEREing and make you able to be Here now?

There are a variety of ways. Here are a few.

The first one that comes to mind is, again, nicely exampled by examining tinnitus. One of the things that is used to alleviate tinnitus is to make a sound-emitting device and put it at the base of the neck. This device then emits the same steady tone that is emitted by the inner ear, or by the mistaken reading of the neurons, or by the lack of filtering, or whatever the heck is really going on (*The Practitioner*, 1992). Whatever the cause, when we meet outside sound with inside sound, we can get the brain to sort of put it in the background and stop Hearing it—sometimes!

And that reduction in distraction allows us to get back to the business of HEREing.

But wait! There's more!

Thinking about that tinnitus-relieving tonal device at the base of someone's neck causing a shift in focus and function reminds me of a documentary called *The Weeping Camel* (*The Story of the Weeping Camel*, 2002).

It was because of *The Weeping Camel* that I came to understand the degree to which sound and music entrain and force change upon the brain.

It was because of *The Weeping Camel* that I came to understand more fully how we function, especially in relation to where we focus our attention. I came to understand how what we Hear changes what we see, changes whether we're internally focused or externally focused, changes whether we feel love or revulsion or complacency.

These changes being so easily forced upon us by the unnoticed sounds in our world is really, really, important!

I'm going to tell you about this movie in order to share my epiphany.

SPOILER ALERT! I'm going to ruin the movie for you because the epiphany comes at the end. So if you don't want me to spoil the fun of discovery, go rent the movie, watch it and come back to this point in the book more aware. But for those of you who want the information now, without doing homework, let's continue.

The Weeping Camel is a documentary. It's about a camel, a mother camel that refuses to accept her calf. The story takes place in Mongolia. Momma camel won't mother her baby, won't feed it, and won't even nurture it with physical contact of any kind. The camel herders try to keep the baby alive while searching for a solution (Davaa and Falorni, 2004).

They know the answer. They just have a challenge enforcing it: it's a problem of progress.

They need a special kind of music doctor, so they go looking. It's the modern age so there aren't many of these special doctors anymore, and for some time their search seems futile. The baby is weakening, bottle-feeding is failing to replace mothering—and then finally, they find the needed musical healer. He comes across the dunes by motorcycle—a sight for saddened eyes—and puts something that looks like it might amplify sound around the neck of the momma camel. He stands a few feet away and begins to play a haunting tone with his unusual wind instrument. The horn's music causes the camel to swoon. The camel literally cries. Tears come out of her eyes; and after weeks of refusing to feed her nearly dead baby, she walks over, nuzzles, and feeds her calf. *She has become externally focused.*

Whatever had gone on for momma camel, her emotions were now changed. She stops perseverating on her own issues, and her feeling of revulsion to her calf shifts and softens. She becomes able to love and open up. The musician's sounds have brought her to the Here and now. She's able to see what's in front of her and to take care of it. In this case, what is in front of her is her baby.

HEARing brought her Here to the place she was meant to be.

All because of a song so deftly played.

This reaction is not unique to camels. It's true in humans, too.

Sound can influence your focus in or out, now or then, up or down.

If you use sound well, it can help you, BE HERE NOW.

What you Hear helps you Hear, Here.

Understand?

Think about it. Think about the times that you had a feeling of sadness, and you were a teenager, and you went and listened to sad music, and it helped you to be really, *really* good and sad. And then, after a few minutes of overindulging in melancholy, maybe you shifted the music a little bit, and got a little happier, and you shifted it a little more, and got a little happier still; then you shifted yet again till you ended up dancing around your room, delighted to be alive.

That is an example of using music well to get out of the then and into the now.

You gave yourself music therapy. You entrained your brain. You went to where it was at, and you brought it somewhere else. HEARing helps you to be Here, in the present, in the moment that you're really in, which is in your room—not in your sadness over the boyfriend you broke up with, or the girlfriend, or whatever was going on for you, but in your room in a happy moment with music playing.

Sound itself is a part of the answer. But it's how we—our brains—Hear the sound that makes it all happen for us. It makes us able to be Here in the present, Here where we're at, and Hear the people around us.

LEADER: DR. RICHARD ALPERT (1931–) renamed Ram Dass (1967) is the author of the culturally influential book *Be Here Now*. The name Ram Dass means servant of God and was given to him in India by Maharaji—a Hindu guru and mystic. Ram Dass and Timothy Leary—a writer and psychologist known for advocating psychedelic drugs—were Harvard professors who researched and personally experimented with psychedelics.

These forays into the mentally distorting world of LSD purportedly introduced the Jewish born atheist doctor to God. Both Leary and Dass (then Dr. Alpert) were dismissed from Harvard in 1963 under controversial circumstances. Shortly thereafter Dass travelled to India where he met Maharaji.

The book *Be Here Now* was a huge success which brought the title phrase into common use. *Be Here Now* so influenced the American hippie generation that it is referred to as a "counterculture bible" and "seminal" to the era.

The book comes in four sections. 1) Autobiographical quest from doctor to spiritually evolving as a yogi; 2) Metaphysical teachings: 3) A manual or cookbook for "how to start down a spiritual path" and 4) Suggested readings.

As mentioned *Be Here Now* had a huge cultural influence on the hippie generation, and many followers of the book followed the yogi Ram Dass. Ram Dass was a Leader of people, but so was his book (Dass, 2010).

In the case of this published work, in many ways, the bigger Leader is not even the book; it's the title.

The title *Be Here Now* is the real influencer as it has been referred to, restated, and reused by many more people than the estimated two million readers who bought the book. Many people who don't even know what, or whom, Ram Dass is will use the phrase and share in its blessing.

A Leader leaves words of love on the path of life for others to listen to, to HEAR, to find, and to follow.

A Leader leaves love notes and continues down the path. Leaders do not need to be there to HEAR the message read. Instead Leaders are HERE wherever they are, when they are there.

Be Here Now is almost all he needed to write.

||||||||||||||||||||||||||||||||||||||||||||| ▲ ▲ ▲ ||||||||||||||||||||||||||||||||||||||||||||||||

All Great Leaders are intentionally Here so they can Hear, You when you get HERE too!

But that's not the whole story.

There's more!

HEARing cannot only tell if you are Here in the Here and now but it can also locate your position, where you are in relation to others. In that sense HEARing is a Leader identifier.

In fact, HEARing is one of your most positional senses.

You probably didn't know this because most of the aspects to HEARing that people believe encompasses all there is to know about HEARing, they learned in grade school and never revamped.

For example, you likely already knew that light has a faster speed of travel than sound (C. Chapman, 2001). You were probably taught that when looking at a noise-making device, you would See it before you would Here it despite the fact that you yourself couldn't detect a difference in arrival time. This explanation may have then been stretched to explain why lightening comes before thunder. You may have been told that counting how many seconds passes after you See lightening until you Hear thunder helps identify how far away the cloud location is that the lightening originated from (Burby, 1999).

You maybe even already know that sound is actually just vibrations in the air, and those waves of vibration go into your ear and wiggle the little hairs inside that we referred to as cilia (Morgan and Bloom, 2006). You likely knew this even before I told you about cilia and tinnitus. Odds are you were taught that air vibrations wiggle the little cilia and they wiggle the neurons, and the neurons phase-lock together and emit a tone. You may even have personified those cilia as a little chorus of heads all lined up in a row singing, "Ooooooo! This tone! Ooooo! This sound! Ooooo! This pitch! Oooooo!" Then followed it with back-up singer neuron groups translating it all into meaning throughout the symphony of your brain.

Finally it may have already been obvious to you that there are many, many places where the translation of sound to meaning can go wrong and be messed up. You may have known all of this. However, you were likely not told it all. I suspect they left out an important piece—a locational reality to the Here in HEARing that most students are never taught.

Sound isn't just vibrations; it also functions to identify depth and position in space.

Sound has shape. It has a type of depth perception. It's like a compass, an auditory compass, in a way. You probably *are* aware of it at some subconscious level; but in the case of positional HEREing you, probably didn't know what you knew.

This may sound like a familiar concept because the one aspect of positional sound detection that you most likely *were* taught refers to distance. For example, in school they often explain the Doppler Effect using the analogy of a train, explaining that when it's coming toward you the pitch of its clanking wheels is higher than when the train is going away (Enderle, Bronzino, and Blanchard, 2005).

So the pitch changes identify location, speed, and direction. But they may never have explained to you that it isn't just *where* the items in your world are and what *they* are doing that your ability to HEAR can detect. When you're paying attention to HEARing and how HEARing functions, you'll also discover where *you* are in relation to others and how *you* move in contrast to *them*.

> *Be sure to put your feet in the right place; then stand firm.*
>
> ~ Abraham Lincoln

In other words, HEARing, H-E-R-E-I-N-G, is about knowing yourself in relation to others.

And so is being a Leader.

Am I Here? Do I Hear where I Here? Is HEARing, Here, important?

Understanding this HEREing concept of relative positioning can lead to auditory existentialism.

This is true both in the physical sense and in the emotional sense.

Physically, we have a different process for recognizing the sound waves that have travelled to us vertically, from the sound waves that have reached us via a horizontal path—up and down versus side to side—each of these is read differently by the brain, and signaled by body-wide processes (Bernstein, 2000). Add to that information the ability to detect, "How fast did it move?" in relation to others, and we achieve locale detection aka *spatial awareness*.

By factoring in what your body is doing and knowing how fast each sound moved towards you, whether it went up, whether it went across, whether it stayed steady or shifted away, you're able to know where you are in relationship to the other things in your world.

This is the piece of sound-related HEREing that people don't usually think about. But they should.

Think about it. Think about it now: "Where is everything else in relationship to me?" Look around and ponder the question.

If you want to be a Great Leader, you have to know about both, *them and you.*

You have to understand the interplay between physical and emotional, between metaphorical and reality. To be a Great Leader is to see the truth behind the concept that each person's physiology becomes their psychology just as their psychology becomes their physiology.

So it follows that to be a Great Leader you must understand the physiology of HEREing as well as the psychology of HEARing. This is because where you are in space mingles with the psychology of your intention and determines what you and your people experience.

As a Leader you have to know both of these HEREing truths.

Though it is true that your perceptions will always be affected by your beliefs, I want to focus more on physiology Here because I already explained the comingling of beliefs in the previous chapter on vision. In fact, I want you to take everything I explained about vision and perception and beliefs in that chapter, and I want you to go ahead and lay that onto every single one of the Leadership Sensibilities as you move throughout the book, because belief distortion always applies.

The senses of being a Leader will always be affected by what you believe, by what the people looking to you for Leadership believe, how and what you then Lead them to come to believe about life, about you, and about themselves.

So just apply that brush of understanding everywhere!

Because I want to talk about something else.

This section is devoted to the focus of HEREing so that you, and your followers, can HEAR.

You have to be Here where people are with their beliefs, with their wishes, with their goals, with their intentions—you have to Hear everybody you're trying to get to follow you Here—you have to know what they *want* in order to give them what they *need*.

Because want is what gets in the way and is always the layer on top of need, which makes it hard for them to See.

Now in order to be the one who Sees and Hears what they need, you have to know, not only what they want, but also where their yearnings are, where their aches are, where their problems are, and why they can't fix it all. And to do that, you have to be able to Hear them when they speak, which means you must get *your* want out of the way, while still holding strong to the goal of helping.

Being a Great Leader requires super human sensibilities.

And even if you can Hear all that, if you don't know how to be H-E-

R-E, fully present and at the ready, while you H-E-A-R them share, you can't Lead anyone, for you will be too busy pushing.

Leaders Lead others to come to where they are, to their Here and now.

To do that you must be able to go where your people are and head back from whence you came.

You need to be able to answer these questions:

Where am I in relation to my people, psychologically and physiologically?

Am I standing in the position that puts me at the front?

Am I the engine, or am I in the middle of the train?

Where am I in relation to the others that would derail me and my team?

This may be easier to imagine if you think of yourself on the stage:

Are you speaking out to an audience of one or many?

Are they all Hearing you, fidgeting, sleeping, jeering?

Can you Hear them Hear you, and know that you are Here?

Sound identifies more than just where you are in space; it identifies where you are in relation to them. And if you want to Lead, you must know if you are Here where they are, or Here where you intend for them to someday be. If you are not at the front of the line, your first job is to get there.

So, as a Leader, you have two goals for HEREing:

One: HEAR their need and learn to fill it, while at the same time taking them where you want them to go.

Two: HEAR if you are HERE in the space you wish to be. Are you at the front? Are you in position? Are you ready to Lead and have you taken the stance that has to be taken?

The only way for you to know if you are in the front is to HEAR where you are in space in relation to others. The only way is to listen.

So far, it is evident that perSEEving requires both sight and sound.

If you rely on Seeing alone, you will misinform yourself because you will get only part of the information.

You See, when you See, you can only See out the front of your head and a little bit to the sides peripherally.

So, you may think you're at the front of the train, because you cannot See behind your head and you are focused at where you want to go. But you may, in fact, be looking at an optical illusion made out of mirrors and smoke. But, with HEREing, since sound can travel through walls and around corners, you actually become aware of your 360-degree environment—the Here that you are in.

When you put them both together, your delusions are harder to engage.

And thus you become more aware of whether or not you are actually ready, whether or not you are actually in the correct position to Lead.

And if the crowd is bigger ahead of you, or there is no one at your back, you've got a ways to go before you pull that whistle on the train and say, "Follow me, Hear. I am, Here."

Chapter Three

SENSE THREE in the SEVEN SENSES of LEADERSHIP

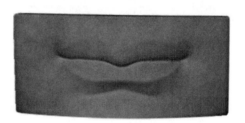

MYTH #6

There are no systems for building
Leaders' brains.

Simply not true. There are steps to being able to do that and the first one is mindset. What type of mindset are you choosing? I suggest you choose a continually expanding one. In other words choose a growth mindset, rather than a static one.

This is how you begin. This is the first step. Open yourself to continual exploration and self-education; add to your experience and your abilities. That's growth. Once you grow, grow more; look for additional opportunities and then open up and add those. Be the best version of you. Step away from the muck and the mire in the world of arguments and stop treading water by engaging in the repetition of unadjusted failed attempts just because you don't want to face your false assumptions and grow into your complete potential. Be more!

To do that your brain needs to process and respond while making completely different choices than it normally would.

True; quick deciding often relies on known answers, but engaging in newness can be done when there is time to make a measured decision. Look forward or back over the experience and contemplate. Toss out the usual answers and seek inspiration.

Getting a TASTE for measured newness is a healthy addiction that grows your mindset. Go for it!

Use the tried and true methods of journal writing, meditation, case-study analysis, and investigative learning. These grow your toolbox of skills, grow your mindset, and enhance your leadership skills ad infinitum. This is because, especially when answer-seeking is done in a less pressured, more relaxed brain state, finding new solutions becomes a habit. This perpetual increasing of the options available for solving a given problem grows a more flexible brain.

A healthy brain is a flexible brain. In fact, it has been said that in the battle of wills, *the most flexible brain wins,* by getting to its goal (S. B. Chapman and Kirkland, 2014). The person with a flexible brain has so many adaptable learned options that they can duck and weave through any obstacle problem course life throws at them. People with robust Leadership qualities are known to engage in these activities more often than those who remain followers (Scouller, 2011).

The system for you to follow in order to become an effective Leader

Here are some clearly defined techniques. These techniques work, because they increase your creativity and maximize the power of your mental flexibility.

1. **Stop venting; it doesn't really help. Venting is an action that gets you talking in circles in order to justify the insurmountable nature of it all. Venting convinces you of the problem you already know you have! Instead:** *Reduce your paragraphs into one or two sentences that clearly define the core of the problem. Look into your memory for anyplace at all—movies, books, YouTube, your own life—wherein you may have encountered a similar situation.* Once you note the problem and align it with a similar remembered one, recall the results of the solution that was employed. At this point, if you have time to contemplate, analyze the story and imagine what needs to be done differently in order to apply an adapted version of that solution to your present moment. Even if the results you

are recalling were bad, it's a place to start. Learn from the mistake and mentally renovate the choice till it's more promising. Now mentally copy what worked and adjust what didn't to fit your present situation. Win or lose, the new attempt becomes food for the next problem-solving fodder. WARNING: if you don't have time for contemplation and need to think quickly, skip this step; move on to the next one immediately.

2. **Stop looking at the broken part in dismay by looking instead at all the available details!** *In whatever fragment of time you may have, open your mind to search out all the details.* Ask nothing more of yourself in this moment. Gather all the bits and pieces of data related to the problem regardless of whether or not they seem important. Get all of the ingredients and do not sift any of them out. Invite your intuition in and get a TASTE for what is happening.

3. **Now return to problem solving!** *Imagine all possible solutions.* If you have to think fast, keep your imagining linear. Look for a solution based on what has worked before using what is available now. However, if you have time, consider your options for a bit longer. The best ideas often come after throwing out lots of obvious solutions. A well-known comedy writer friend of mine used to jot down fifty jokes and then throw out the paper and say, "Ah! Now it's getting funny!" And he was right. Genius is often covered up by easily accessible habits. This is because the obvious solutions are your first inclination to try, but if they were working you would have used them already and the problem would be gone. So dig deeper. You need to get past your habits before you can get to the here-to-fore unknowns, the surprises, the priceless, unexpected jewels.

4. **Hold your horses and consider the escape!** *New solutions breed new consequences. Make a game plan to deal with the ripple effect of your choice.* Never underestimate the power of change. If you

don't have time to think of everything, think of what you can. Just the intention to be thorough can help you imagine the cascade of change this action will cause.

5. **Get galloping and act! But pay attention to the hairs on your neck!** *Logic is useful but, like those first fifty jokes, logic is subject to the obvious. In order to grow you have to listen to your instincts as well.* Instincts aren't really so different from logic. They are, in fact, a composite of fast logic based on experience and genetic coding. The more experienced a Leader you are, the more your instincts will Lead you to the right decision. So, the more willing you are to make decisions, the more experienced you become, and the better you are.

Decisions are an action step. Take the action and step.

Yes, there is a system of steps for growing your Leadership Sensibilities by practicing your decision-making skills.

You can make it if you're open to it.

It may feel stressful, especially if you have to make this choice quickly. Stress is part of stretching, but be aware of how stress has affected your thinking in the past. Adapt the steps to suit your thinking style; make sure your mind is as clear as possible while considering your options.

Get comfortable with fleeting low levels of stress by knowing that it is normal and potentially beneficial. Get excited to be growing. Panic shuts down the executive functions of the frontal lobes and is never a creative decision-maker. So don't FEED the fear.

The secret to a flexible brain is simple: Try new things and don't resist change. Resistance leads to panic which results in flight, fight, or freeze.

Instead take a deep, slow breath. Imagine the TASTE of victory, set an intention, and choose.

Finally, just remember—it's all in your head.

SENSE THREE

TASTE TESTING

Have you ever been about to put something new into a recipe—something you wouldn't normally put in—but this time you are forced into creating a new combination because, perhaps, you ran out of the usual ingredients? Perhaps your success was imperative and you couldn't just give up and go for fast food; or perhaps you thought, "Well, I like to cook soup and there's not much in the house. I'll just have to be creative!"

So you imagined the flavor.

You asked yourself, "Will this particular"—let's say it's asparagus—"will it work?" And then you tasted it with your mind.

Have you ever tried that? Have you ever tried to imagine the taste of asparagus bubbling in a broth? Have you ever brought it into your mental mouth, smacked your actual lips a little bit, let it linger in your brain's sensory strip, and then mentally mixed it with the other ingredients that you've already put in the pot? Have you adjusted the flavor to suit your preferences with a little spice? Perhaps it's lemon pepper.

Think lemon pepper.

If you have never done this before, try it now as you read.

Think, lemon pepper, asparagus, and add a little tomato sauce? Do it. Right now. And then throw in a little cayenne pepper for zip. Now taste it. Swallow. YUM!? Or YUCK!?

Let's assume YUM! Now! Just before you're done, notice that it needs something. Smack your lips again, this time searching for the answer. Roll your eyes up and to the right to enhance your ability to imagine. Lick your lips, search your mind, move your tongue about in your mouth, think! What is it? Ah! It needs a substance. That's what it is. It needs some chunk. You know this because your teeth are almost craving the ability to chew. But what kind of chunk exactly; chips? No. Not chips.

Think! Tastefully think, "Beef? Maybe! Steak? Stewing beef? Nooo... something else?"

Okay, let's assume that beef isn't working for you. Somehow, the idea of it leaves your mouth feeling deader than just a minute ago, less salivating. So, instead, you think, "Hmmm... Sausage? Maybe ground-up pork sausage?" And now you feel the juices come into the sides of your mouth, and you can taste the sausage, the tomato, the lemon pepper, and the asparagus—broken into little chunks of soft green mush—and now you've made a soup without ever lifting a spoon.

And it's delicious.

You know it will be delicious if you make it this way, because you already have. This is the art and science of projection.

You can now happily put these ingredients into a pot, positive that the tastes will come together exactly as you desire.

That kind of imagining and understanding is what it takes to make choices as a Leader (Kouzes and Posner, 2012). You will have to combine the flavors of many different types of people. You'll have to be able to see which ones make you salivate, and which ones don't. You have to know who complements whom and how they interact with each other. Most of us have done it at some point in our life.

We've been setting the table for a party or a family gathering, and we've thought, "Actually, Uncle Joe's flavor doesn't mingle well with Cousin Ned's. I'm going to put them farther apart from each other, and I'm going to put Aunt Mary in between them, because she has a tendency to blend and sweeten everything." Aunt Mary is like the tomato sauce in our soup!

In life, some people function that way—they're the connectors, they're the blenders, they're the broth in the soup. Some people are the meat—the crumpled-up pork or the chunky beef, while others are like dessert—sweet and bright and full of celebration—and you bring them in for just that reason—to celebrate.

Being a Leader is about making deals.

And a Great Leader knows how to cook a deal.

IIIIIIIIIIIIIIIIIIIIIIIIIIIIIIIIIIIIIIIIIIIII ▼ ▼ ▼ IIIIIIIIIIIIIIIIIIIIIIIIIIIIIIIIIIIIIIIIIIIIIII

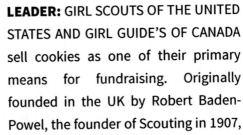

LEADER: GIRL SCOUTS OF THE UNITED STATES AND GIRL GUIDE'S OF CANADA sell cookies as one of their primary means for fundraising. Originally founded in the UK by Robert Baden-Powel, the founder of Scouting in 1907, The World Association of Girl Guides and Girl Scouts has grown into the largest voluntary movement dedicated to women and girls in the world (Reynolds, 1991). They represent ten million women and girls from 146 countries around the world. And though not every participating Girl Guide/Scout country sells cookies, and though the cookie recipes are quite varied, Girl Guide/Scout Cookies are internationally famous and have estimated annual sales worth $800 million in the USA alone.

Like with many Leader stories, the claim to fame has gotten manipulated, shared, and re-shared over the years. For example, in Canada the birth of the cookie is attributed to a Leader in Regina, Saskatchewan, who baked and packaged the first cookies as a means of raising money for camping equipment and uniforms. This story dates back to 1927 and is nationally recognized as true. However, in 1917 the Mistletoe Troop from Muskogee, OK, stopped kissing for money and started selling sugar cookies instead. According to the American history of cookies, these were the original Girl Guide cookies (Girlscoutsorg, 2016). In Singapore *the great cookie sale* was launched in 1994 and no one tries to say they came up with the cookie concept.

Leaders are products. They brand themselves and share the nutrition of their message. They watch the market and rewrite the recipe where necessary. Girl Guide Cookies are a highly successful version of Leadership by branding. Girl Guide cookies are Leaders that keep you salivating supported by volunteers around the globe.

But cookies, like Leaders, do not have to be the product to affect an influence; they can be an adjunct, a subtle part of the ambiance tipping the scales and making you salivate enough to buy… a house or an idea. For example, realtors suggest baking chocolate chip cookies to make a house smell so good you can TASTE its warmth. A Great Leader is similarly often part of the ambience that changes the flavor of things. They ooze the Taste of confidence, vision, and clarity and make their ideas desirable.

||||||||||||||||||||||||||||||||||||||||||||| ▲ ▲ ▲ |||||||||||||||||||||||||||||||||||||||||||||||||

TASTE, TESTS!

Taste is bigger than the receptors on the surface of your tongue. Just as human beings are more than their clothes and the surface image they portray, Taste—like all the senses so far—is more complex and valuable than what you were taught in grade school.

Taste actually Tests and Retests our reality through comparative analysis and imagination.

Taste is strongly influenced by Smell, but we'll get to that in the next section. It's also influenced by vision and sound, which we've talked about.

Hearing and Feeling the crunch or the soft "swish-moosh" of a food can strongly influence the way a thing will Taste.

All your senses working together (correctly or incorrectly) build your experience. They can create an image of shape, which is read or misread by the brain, even in relation to food. This dissonant or harmonic union of abilities tells you what you are Tasting and can even suggest to you that you're munching on a square or a triangle, despite the fact that you don't know what either of those might taste like (Martin, 2013).

In fact, this mix-up, this magnificent confusion of our senses, has a name. Synesthesia. (Cytowic, 2012)

We talked about synesthesia a little bit—in vision and sound—so now let's add Taste to the collection of senses and bring the importance of comparative Tasting home. For some people synesthesia is just a rainbow of colors emitted by sound, but for others, who taste squares and circles and triangles, synesthesia is exactly what I described earlier: a spatial disorder of the mouth.

These people are Taste Testing in a very unique and uncommon way. Interesting, huh?

I met a person who said, "Sorry; I can't eat this broth. It has wayyyy too many diamonds poking my mouth." The weird part is I understood him, because I am a Leader with brain science in my head. This is the gift I wish to share with you—an understanding of the differences in nature's design.

People like that *Diamond Soup Man* are not just "out of the box" thinkers; they are literally "in a different box" from you. It is up to you to See into "their world." You can't Lead people who are different from you by arguing or calling them crazy. And you can't Lead people who are the same as you, because people who are the same as you don't need your vision; they already have it.

You *can* shun differences, I suppose, and pretend they don't matter, like shunning a food and calling it YUCKY!

BUT...

Though these different people may not be your Taste or to your liking, if they see value in your teachings, they may be your greatest allies. And you can Lead them. So I suggest you learn to like them.

If you admire their difference and Lead them with acceptance and love, they will follow and add to your knowledge of people. You and they can become complementary ingredients, invaluable parts of each other's sensory system network.

You can start by Tasting what they Taste. You can do this if you use your imagination, Tastefully. But to do that you must gather a little more knowledge on how.

So we are back to the beginning. Learning to understand that Taste is more than just a function of the buds upon your tongue. Taste is a function of the brain and the body decoding incoming messages from the influences of the world we live in. It is a function of combining life's signals into a comprehensive message of existence (Brillat-Savarin, 1925).

True; the flavor of life is brought together in the mouth, in the gut, and in the brain. However, we humans are just the blender of experience. What you actually Taste begins with an expectation based on an idea that is brought to you by the world you live in.

So, let's go there, to the beginning of this world.

Like the peoples of our earth clustering into different cultural groups, Taste buds cluster on different points of your tongue for different sensations of Taste (H. A. Smith, Blecha, and Sternig, 1966). When you were a child in school—if you missed this class, go ahead and look up a picture on the Internet so you can follow along—you were probably taught that at the back of the tongue are the Taste buds for bitter; and on the sides of the tongue are the Taste buds for sour; at the tip of the tongue are the Taste buds for salty and sweet; and in the center of the tongue—not many Taste buds at all. This probably left you with the impression that all Tasting was done in the mouth (Rhoades and Bell, 2009).

And then, one day you burnt your mouth on a hot cup of soup when you were a child and part of your tongue became numb. So you thought, "Yes, in fact, I can't Taste as well, so they must be right. Taste happens on the tongue." However, a year or so later you got a cold, and somebody said to you, "You won't be able to Taste as well because of your cold. It's stuffing up your nose and you can't smell. So therefore, you can't Taste." (Ovalle and Nahirney, 2013)

Suddenly, life was confusing. You added that bit of information and thought, "Ok, so Taste is in the mouth, on the tongue, and it's also, a little bit, to do with maybe the expectation created by smell." Then came the day when you burnt the roof of your mouth and didn't bother your tongue at all, and still, your Taste was affected. Somebody said to you, "Oh, that's because some of your Taste buds were burnt." They handed you something resembling watered-down baby poo to drink and ease the pain. Your mental association with feces caused you to Taste it on sight and you started to gag. And now, even though no one in grade school ever mentioned your eyes or the roof of your mouth, you're becoming educated, made more aware, that your face (eyes, mouth and nose) is a very big deal in relation to Taste (Shinghal, 2002).

This is generally as far as people go in understanding Taste and Taste sensations. I want to take you farther, into the brain.

But first, let's categorize the various types of Taste Testing sensors.

The ones we talk about most identify sweet, sour, salty, bitter; something called umami (Mouritsen and Styrbk, 2014), which is sort of that meaty taste, or that cheesy taste, that you get when you bite into a good steak or cheeseburger and the newly evolved oleogustus which is the taste of fat (Running CA, Craig BA, Mattes RD, 2015). When you think about the people you Lead, you may be able to categorize them similarly. Put some of them in the "sweet" pile, others in the "sour" pile, and some in the "salty" pile. This is a common way of thinking, so much so that these words have made their way into our descriptions of personalities.

Like, "He's the salt of the earth," or, "What spicy characters they had." Or "She leaves a bitter taste in the mouth." (Brand, 2004)

It's okay to put people in the "bitter" pile, the "sour" pile, the "meaty" pile, the "anything" pile. But as you do this, just as with Taste, you're going to have to become very aware of the subtleness of blending. Know that all Tastes are good as long as they are correctly blended into their part of the simmering soup, the symphony of sensations.

And that's why we began with the soup reference: Because when you're cooking up a stew or a soup, or baking a cake, for goodness' sakes, when you're combining anything, it's very important to recognize how one thing affects another and turns it into something else.

All things influence the Taste, the Taste Test and all accompanying decisions meant to create a transformation of what is True—about You and Them.

A good example would be colors. You have primary colors, but when you blend them together, they become a different color entirely (Schopenhauer and Runge, 2012). And that's what happens when you blend people: Different people emerge and are born from the blending of the ones that you put together.

So, just like in your soup, you have ingredients. The ingredients alone are not soup. It's the *combination* of the ingredients that creates what we call soup, which is a brand new thing with a personality all of its own.

However, even though it has a personality, it also has the various aspects and Tasteful representations of each and every ingredient.

And Tasting this kind of versatility is a skill you have to have to be a Great Leader: You must be able to look out at your people, Taste each and every one of them (figuratively, of course!) and blend them together appropriately—sometimes leaving some out, and sometimes over including others because they represent a stronger binding chemical to the whole (Pringle, 2008).

Now, if while reading this you forgot about "imagination" (or believe you lack one), you might say, "How am I going to do that based on Taste? I Lead with my head and Taste is in the mouth." But it isn't, you see. Signals and saliva and food etc. are in the mouth. Taste is in the brain!

And since, as you just confirmed, that's where we do all our thinking and decision making, our head is also the place from which we get our Leadership Sensibilities!

So, now, let's go to the head, of Taste!

Taste buds are actually little receptors on the tongue that take the chemical information of the food you're eating and pass it to your brain so that *your brain* can tell you what you're Tasting (Kratz and Siegfried, 2010).

The brain performs a Test and then tells you what you Taste!

The nerves that are involved in passing that informational Taste Test are the facial nerve, the hypoglossal nerve, and the glossopharyngeal nerve (Haines, 2010).

Let's break it down for clarity. The facial nerve is mostly involved closer to the tip of your tongue where sweetness sits—sort of! It doesn't really sit; it goes into the receptors and signals the taste buds to signal your brain and tell it about the degree of sweetness detected (Conn, 2008).

The hypoglossal nerve is a motor nerve that helps move the food to be tasted into position (Champney, 2015), and the glossopharyngeal nerve brings the messages from the throat area and the palate (throat and palate may not fit your concept of Taste-Testing-Mouth but add it now; it's okay to grow) to the brain (Allan Siegel and Sapru, 2010).

Eventually, through a bunch of feedback loops, all this information ends up in your cognitive centers; all this cooperative signal passing happens in order to reach your awareness, so that you can Taste.

Tasting takes a lot of nerve.

So before I move on, let's talk a little bit more about nerves.

Let's talk about the trigeminal nerve because it's involved in pain and temperature and touch (Calvert and DeVere, 2010). I want you to see how all these systems would come together and create a sensation— not just of the Taste of the food but of the shape of the food, which contributes to Taste, texture, and satisfaction.

Texture matters! Keep that in mind as you Lead people. If your texture is off—too brittle or too soft—and you don't give your message the right shape, it falls flat and people will refuse to eat it (Jacobs, Schimmel, Masson, and Harvill, 2015).

Like cereal: If you let the cereal get soggy it just doesn't *taste* as good. And your children—the ones you hope to Lead into a good breakfast— will refuse to eat it.

Take care of your shape, texture, flavor, and awareness of others. Take care of what you put out and take in; Leadership follows (Maxwell, 2007).

Trust yourself. Hone, improve, and grow; but also know that you are fully equipped.

As your brain gets involved in Taste Testing, it's also seeking to decide whether or not it's detected poison. Whether it's Tasting something flavorful and joyful and emotionally pleasing, or whether it should spit it out and throw up. To make that decision, we don't just use our instinctive systems put in place by evolution. We use our memory. So pay attention and remember more. Brains add more and more information to their files the more focused you become. To be a Great Leader you must give your brain more to work with so that it, and therefore you, can compare and contrast with what's come before (April, Macdonald, and Vriesendorp, 2000).

Taste, Test, and Decide. This is a must in order to make accurate choices and Tasteful decisions.

People, like food, have been overly processed. Finding their core value can take work and selectivity.

For example, as a result of changes in our diet and the avoidance of toxins, we've evolved to sort of neutralize our human bitter sensitivity. This has made it so that we've sort of mutated, as compared to other animals, and ended up with a reduced ability to detect or be revolted by bitterness, which used to be paired occasionally with the warning signal for poison.

Thus, as evolution comes into play, Taste Testing becomes harder and more important to refine.

I could go on, and on, and on. I could talk more about all of the receptors and the calcium and the sodium, G-protein coupling which enables you to change and evolve as well as the various chemical components of everything (Giraldo and Pin, 2011), but too much science can be misleading and make you believe that what you know is static and fully defined.

Nothing is ever static and fully defined, especially not Taste.

Taste is an enormously complex function.

As a Leader you should look at the world that you're trying to reach and teach, Lead and motivate, and ask yourself, "Is this a salty group? Did I walk onto the stage and look out at a salty group? And if so, shall I be the salt of the earth with them? Or shall I Lead them by blending in some meatiness, a little pepper, a touch of sweet?"

It may sound very basic and almost silly, but it isn't. When we take something to our natural inclination of understanding, which in this case is our five basic senses (I'm going to add two more), it becomes fun, comprehendible, and Tasty!

When we do that, we go to ourselves and we signal our instincts. We say, "Come with me instincts. Help me to understand how to blend these people, how to take this group and turn them into one thing; come with me and use these wonderful human ingredients to make a soulful soup."

We say that, and more.

You know, there's something personal about Taste, something almost judgmental that calls us to be wary.

The very act of Tasting implies Testing.

In order to Taste there is a need to ascertain the difference between good and bad. We must do this or the poison meter in our brain will atrophy and die (Schalley and Khlentzos, 2007). But ascertaining poison isn't the same as believing it is unchangeable and can't be recombined into nutrition. This limitation is caused by judgment and has nothing to do with Taste except in how the beliefs shape your experience.

> *"The way to entice people into cooking is to cook delicious things."*
>
> ~ *Yotam Ottolenghi*

There are various sensations that can come as a result of particles in people and foods, and a result of the combined reactions in our mouth and our brain and our body. There's more than we've talked about. There's pungency and coolness and numbness that can be stimulated by Taste and belief.

There's "you" and "me" and our ideas that make "we."

Everything that "we" experience in the very personal sense of Taste is multilayered and interconnected.

But despite that interconnection, Taste is a very personal sense.

In fact, I see Taste and Touch as being in their own category, so I have coined the term, "Personal Senses."

When you *Hear* something, you know it is either a mistake of imagination and/or physiology or you heard it from out there in the world, and then it came in.

When you *See* something, it is similar. You know you're looking at something out there and bringing it in. When you visualize, you know you're inventing it inside your head but that it's separate from out there.

And though these are very inclusive senses, the experience of them stays in and about your head.

However, when you *Taste*, it grounds you in yourself, blends you together and stirs in your beliefs, in order to be experienced in your body.

So, if you ask yourself, "What is that tomato and that carrot going to Taste like together?" the combination of ingredients becomes one thing.

Taste becomes intimately You, Me, and Us individually.

Taste becomes a sensation in the body—not just in the head.

And Taste Testing becomes a way to recreate the recipe.

So now, we're taking our senses and we're moving them into our wholeness of being; we're moving them everywhere.

This is how you want to Lead people: You want to create a flavor in the world that creates a Taste for you, so that you can become one of the ingredients in everybody's soup. And you want to Taste good enough to make everybody's soup better.

You cannot do that if you don't know how to be both the primary Taste while at the same time stay able to congeal all of the various flavors of the world.

Taste Testing over and over and over again strengthens your Leadership Sensibilities and your ability to Lead with Taste.

Chapter Four

SENSE FOUR in the SEVEN SENSES of LEADERSHIP

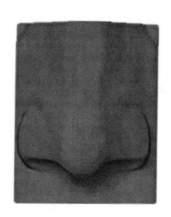

MYTH #7

True Leaders are born, not made.

The question of Leaders being born rather than made is that long-argued nature versus nurture debate on what came first the neuron or its state.

Regardless of what you believe, the truth is, all brains change, all the time.

Though successful Leaders are believed to have increased grey matter in the brain locations used to control decision making and memory (Puri, Amma, and Devi, 2014), and though this might give Leaders an edge with quick logic and visionary-like choices, since neuronal constructs are self-molding organisms, we have no way of knowing if the extra grey matter developed before the Leadership skills or after.

If you think the function and geography of the adult brain is finished forming —think again—literally. And while you are rethinking, your brain, which has the ability to change itself, changes itself. With each new experience your brain self-renovates; and this happens in every aspect from structure, to function, to emotional regulation, and personality creation (Schultz and Schultz, 2016).

People who are open to new concepts, experiences, or procedures generally expose themselves to rich information sources such as print, Internet searches, television, and interactive conferences. As a result they build denser neural networks. Denser neural networks increase the complexity of the brain (Arbib, 2003). A complex, yet organized and purposefully focused brain leads to the birth of a possible Leader—or more accurately said—to the construction of Leadership material.

Thus, it follows that people averse to information, newness, concepts, abstractions, or interactive discussions have more impoverished neural networks and are likely to evolve either as followers, or as inflexible, poorly equipped "Fake Leaders" hiding behind the act of controlling others, despite how those "others" are impacted.

Fortunately, if you wish it, an aversion to newness and complexity can be replaced with the simple willingness to try.

Step 1. Be open and willing, on purpose.

You truly can rewire your mind by renovating your mindset, and in the process you can definitely become a more effective Leader.

In fact with a constant thirst for knowledge, you can do even better than that. You can go all the way.

From follower to Leader, from Leader to Great Leader, From Great Leader to Stupendous Leader, From Stupendous Leader to the Sky is the Limit Leader with a full set of Leadership Sensibilities!

In the case of skill evolution, it's all about growth and longevity.

SENSE FOUR

THE ODOR OF ADORE!

The smell of success when it comes to Leadership requires that a group, a tribe, a few people *choose you to Lead them*. The smell of success requires that they choose to hang on your every word, to listen to your advice, to understand through your eyes, to Hear through your ears, to perSEEv, be Here now, in your company, and Taste the soup of life that you throw into your pot of "how to."

When people choose a Leader, they often say that they resonate with that Leader's words, with that Leader's approach, look, style, energy, and spirit. The chemical messenger for this resonance, creating a response to some invisible force, comes through the sense of Smell.

In other words, the Smell of success in a Leader can be thrown out there like a chemical pheromone, like a pheromone of love or a pheromone of hate.

Pheromones are like an airborne hate virus or love bug, changing the minds of everyone they touch.

People choose their Leaders out of fear or out of love. This section is about the sense of Adore. I want to help you send out the message: "Adore me!" I have no interest in teaching you to get better at the message, "Fear me!" So I'm not going to give "fear" any digital space or teach to the chemical messenger that creates it.

Thus, I call this sense, *"**The ODOR of ADORE**."*

To help you understand, I'm going to talk about three things: The chemical messenger of smell, how the sense of Smell works, and what the heck is a pheromone? Why is it different from the chemical messenger scent of say—a chocolate chip cookie?

I will give you a hint: cookie chemicals stimulate salivation and make you want to eat; pheromones are hormones secreted by another person. They are undetectable to you and make you want to snuggle up. Both are delivered to your brain via your Smeller, the nose.

The last sense I talked about was Taste, and both Taste and Smell are chemical senses. They're called that because they detect chemicals in the environment. The difference between Smell and Taste is that Smell can detect chemical messengers from very far away in our environment, whereas Taste mostly happens when something is "placed" in the mouth (Mancall and Brock, 2011). Smell, therefore, has a strong relationship with Taste—they're similar. I've often thought (and who knows, maybe someone will read this next sentence and decide to do it) that there is probably a way to create a Smell food that actually supplies nutrition to the body. If I figure out how to do it—how to Smell my Vitamin B12 and not have to eat and gain weight—I'm sure I'll be extremely rich! But for now, let's just talk about what is actually known in regards to those chemical messengers that float about in the air.

Basically, chemicals—vaporized Odor molecules—are floating around making you do things reflexively. You will experience emotions, sensual turn-ons and salivation (Khanorkar, 2011)—especially if you're walking outside of places like a Kentucky Fried Chicken franchise—to name just a few. So unconscious is our response to Smell that restaurants learned to fan their Odors outdoors to make you hungry and gain sales. This cause-and-effect connection to your behavior happens even when it's too subtle to consciously detect. Perfume and food marketers are really good at throwing all their chemical messengers around for you to deal with. You may not buy, but you will respond!

How does it work?

Chemical messengers reach the roof of each of your nostrils and dissolve the mucous in there (Bear, Connors, and Paradiso, 2007). By the way, what I'm talking about right now is just your sense of Smell. It's a little different when we're talking about pheromones, so let's just think in terms of Smell itself for now. Underneath the mucous in the olfactory epithelium—I'm not very good at saying that, but fortunately, you're reading so you can just imagine its pronunciation—are specialized receptor cells called olfactory receptor neurons and they detect Odor (Menini, 2009). They decide what these different chemical messengers mean, put the codes together, and tell you what you're Smelling.

And here's something cool: A trillion smells—it used to be thought it was only ten thousand—but a trillion smells can be identified by the human nose (Yeoman, McMahon-Beattie, Fields, Meethan, and Albrecht, 2015).

A trillion! Isn't that amazing?

At every turn we are made up of more than we can even fathom, and in this regard the Odor of Adore is no exception.

Okay, I'm going to take you quickly through this. The olfactory receptors give the information to the olfactory bulbs at the back of the nose (Nevid, 2014). Now the olfactory bulbs have these sensory receptors that are actually part of the brain, so the messages go directly to the target brain center. That is what separates the boys from the girls, or the senses from each other—the nose from the eyes, the ears, and the mouth (Linden, 1998).

The nose has a direct route with no filtering.

The nose is special, or at least the sense of Smell is, because the most primitive brain center—the limbic system—is where your influence of emotions and memories come together, and your sense of Smell can go directly there (Pepe and Consulting, 2000).

Now, with every other sense, it's different. With every other sense, the signals travel along circuitous pathways to *make their way* into your emotions. The information makes its way there *after* having been filtered and sort of thought about, believed about.

But the sense of Adore happens *before* you think. It stimulates emotions and memories before your frontal lobes—the part of you that filters and decides what things mean—get involved (Freberg, 2009). How that plays out as important for you is that often Smell can be the strongest trigger to repulsion or attraction or memory formation; and if you're a Leader, you want to know that.

How 'you' Smell determines how 'they' feel about you.

If you Smell afraid, they feel distrust, empathy, anger, fear, etc. They do not feel Adoring!

IIIIIIIIIIIIIIIIIIIIIIIIIIIIIIIIIIIIIIIIIIII ▼ ▼ ▼ IIIIIIIIIIIIIIIIIIIIIIIIIIIIIIIIIIIIIIIIIIIIIIIIII

LEADER: RUBY BRIDGES (1954~) was a 6-year-old African-American girl who in 1960 helped to integrate the all-white schools of New Orleans. Although she was a young child, she braved the faces of angry white citizens yelling and screaming at her while keeping their children away from her "contamination", every day. She was the only black girl to come to that school, and because a black girl was in school the other moms kept their children away. So she was the only student. She was escorted to and from to keep her safe. Despite the cruel words of the white people that stood outside the school every morning and afternoon, she faced them with compassion and emerged unscathed, physically or emotionally (Coles, 2010).

A white teacher from the North named Barbara Henry helped and encouraged her. Her teacher, her mother Lucille, and her own quiet strength eventually broke down a century-old barrier forever, a pivotal moment in the civil-rights movement.

This true story was made into a movie in 1998 (Palcy, 1998). And though Ruby Bridges was the Leader of integration in New Orleans and a Leader who established The Ruby Bridges Foundation, which promotes values of respect, tolerance, and appreciation of all differences, it was the movie itself that became the Leader for me (Donaldson, 2009).

Once a story is made into a movie, at some level it must be changed to fit into the time frame and the needs of the medium, and as such it lies to us. When filmmakers are forced into that conundrum, the important piece to get right is the "spirit" of the Leader's message. I cannot speak for whether or not this happened in this particular movie, but I can say that the movie version of Ruby's psychiatrist Robert Coles and his words of admiration, which I am directly quoting from the movie in the following paragraph, inspired my commitment to finding strength through faith and purpose as I moved forward in the world. Because these words led me to a place of congruence and understanding, I will share them with you now:

"And so I learned that a family and a child under great stress and fear could show exquisite dignity and courage because of their moral and religious values, and because they had a definite purpose in what they were trying to accomplish. This purpose made them resilient. I couldn't figure out the source of this resilience because I had only worked with well-to-do children who had nothing to work hard for, no reason pushing them to accomplish anything. So now I see that the issue is not stress but stress for what purpose? Having something to believe in protected Ruby from psychiatric symptoms and gave her a dignity and a strength that is utterly remarkable." (Palcy, 1998)

▲ ▲ ▲

Find Your Odor to Adore!

In order to Smell someone deeply enough that you might know whether or not you resonate with them, it is true that all your sensory centers do have to get involved and work cooperatively.

Your frontal lobes do get involved, so your beliefs do come into play.

But in that initial hit—in that fastest-moving-Smell-messenger hit going straight to the brain and letting you know whether to run, or whether to hide, or whether to move towards somebody—everything happens faster than thought. The message of Adore goes to your emotions and changes you before you can analyze and decide.

In the other sense chapters, I suggested you apply the concept of vibrations and frequencies being first decoded and then passed over long hurdle-ridden pathways traversing the brain, before being filtered through your beliefs so that you could perSEEv your reality, to all the senses.

But now I'm telling you: Apply it differently.

Because it is different.

With Sight, and with Sound, and with Taste, the messages do have to pass through these various pathways in the brain, and there are many places where signals can break down and be reconfigured erroneously. It's different with Smell.

Smell, Odor, Adoration, are direct pathways, as long as we don't block them.

You can respond to Smell and not know it. It can hit your limbic system and give you an emotion or a memory before you think. This is an important point. That's why I'm repeating it.

Now, it's true. Odor signals will also go to your thalamus and many other places in the brain; but this one piece of information, this direct route of connection, is invaluable—life changing.

How do you make Odor into Adore? How do you turn this knowledge into something that affects a human being purposefully?

What a great question! It's a question that has been pondered by many, especially in the arena of romantic love and sexual attraction.

That is, other than women attempting to increase the population by wearing the smell of pumpkin and lavender together in order to attract men because these scents are supposed to cause more blood flow to the penis (Andrea Siegel, 1999), which is often misread as Adoration by men and women around the globe. Other than that, science and the sexes aren't very advanced in the art of manipulating Smells for humanity's benefit. However, I want you to really understand the concepts surrounding the Odor of Adore because they are a very important piece in controlling behavior—the behavior that you emit yourself, and then the follower's reaction to it.

Let me give you an example using children.

When you work with a child who's having a tantrum, you can sometimes stop the tantrum simply by having them Smell something that makes them feel comfortable, that makes them feel happy—a Smell they're particularly fond of. There are certain Smells that meltdown professionals have decided are the best for tantrum cessation: banana, strawberry, and a few others (T. Smith and Miller, 2014).

But everybody's an individual—we all react differently. So, if you are having a tantrum, experiment with Smell, and you'll be surprised at how powerful it can be. Smell fills up your sensory path and talks to your emotions. It's part of what's made perfume and aroma industries so happy.

The important point here is that your sense of Smell causes you to react first and think later. It is part of what tells you if something is dangerous, if it's poisonous, or if it's desirable. And it happens so quickly that it could also be part of what makes people Adore or despise their Leaders.

Resonance is responsible for connecting.

Odor is related to resonance and Adoration.

And that makes Leaders of whom people say, "I don't know what it is about him, but he's just so attractive. He's so exciting. He's so enigmatic. I can't take my eyes off him."

When a Leader is referred to as having "IT." I believe what is meant is "That Leader has the ability to 'turn on' his chemical messengers."

Understand that chemical messengers pass way beyond our bodies—out into the crowd, out into the group. If you are strong in your ability to send your message through a chemical messaging system, like the olfactory bulbs, you are going to be able to create a kind of reciprocal Adoration, from and for, your crowd.

Sadly, nobody's figured out how to market or teach creating the Odor of Adore on purpose; but some people do it naturally. And if it can be done naturally, it can be cultivated.

I do believe that that this skill is related to innate instincts and a predisposition for high levels of pheromone production. But I also believe that "turning it on!" is related to Adoring first.

Pheromone production is slightly controversial when it comes to human beings. We know that pheromones work with animals.

We do have various newer studies that say that, "Ooh! Yes! Look! Proof! Proof! There actually are pheromones that pass between the man and the woman, the woman and the man."

Previously, the strongest evidence of pheromone signaling between humans was discovered in the late 1990s, and it was about the menstrual cycles of women living together and how they tended to synchronize. The belief was it happened because of the chemical messengers that were released in the sweat of the women at the time of menses. These chemical messengers, these little bits of information that are passed in the air and that we sniff in, have a very powerful effect on our physiology (Joseph, 2001).

This much we are certain of; though we may not know how to control our creation of the Odor of Adore, we do know that the Odor creates the Adore. Understand, all things in life revolve around perpetually reinforced feedback loops. Therefore, the odds are, an intentionally chosen act of Adoring can create the Odor!

Please do not confuse this with the desperately clung-to-act-of-wanting-someone with Adoration! They are total opposites.

And if you need proof for what I am saying ... well...

I don't put a lot of faith in studies. I prefer results, and the scientific method often prevents these. However, I do like to share information, and there have been some other studies about how pheromone production affects us. For example, women's hypothalamic neurons were activated when they smelled different chemicals from the chemicals that activated men. When women smelled something more like testosterone, but not estrogen, they lit up. And with the men, it was the opposite (Rathus, 2006), (Mucignat-Caretta, 2014). And, yes, this information can lead one to wonder if same-sex attraction is a different—non-procreating desire stimulated by different functioning in these hypothalamic neurons (McAnulty and Burnette, 2006). And that is the thing about questions. They lead to answers that lead to questions and send us searching for the horizon of our own perspectives.

> *"Until you walk a mile in another man's moccasins you can't imagine the smell."*
>
> ~ Robert Byrne

Leaders know when to ask, when to answer and when to just assume so they can act!

Regardless of what we're discovering, there is one thing we could probably always have known if only we had looked with a willingness to assume and act. And that one thing is, since pheromones travel, like your sense of Smell, and can go straight to the brain without first being analyzed, likely: if you can turn them on, you can actually physically Touch your people, from way up there on the stage (Wied and Keep, 2012).

Pheromones zip about in the air, they are breathed into the nose, and then head straight for the area of the brain that likes to like, and want, love, and hate, fear, and Adore things.

And, guess what!? No matter which experience you experience, you change. And they change. They become attracted to you and you become attracted to them. You are now a new soup, completely chemically different—emotionally affected, without any *initial* control over your feelings or reflexive behavior—and that is important to understand.

Fortunately, the frontal lobe's ability to control and redirect follows quick enough behind this phenomenal pheromone effect, that if you understand the science, you can cause an audience response and still remain you, by restoring your own balance faster than the eye can see (Coon and Mitterer, 2008).

Smell strongly influences Taste. If you want people to have a Taste for you, I suggest you Lead with the Odor of Adore.

And on an obvious note: Don't risk causing allergies and offending people by hiding your scent with chemicals that are going to erase who you really are. Send your scent to them in such a way that they enjoy your company. Watch your hygiene. Have fresh breath, armpits, hair, and cloths. If you want them to have a Taste for you as they Smell you, you can't let your hygiene go by the wayside!

Don't just spritz; shower.

The Smell of success Smells like good intentions, not manmade chemicals over week-old underwear.

Remember Odor all on its own is just a Smell.

Unless a system is damaged we are all subject to the "wanted and unwanted" effects of pheromones and Smell. In fact, there's a chance that we're subject to the emotions affected by Smell even if we can't Smell the Smell. This would be true if the pathway to our limbic system is undamaged while the one to our awareness has broken down.

Additionally, the cells that operate in order for you to Smell renew every thirty to sixty days (Martin, 2013). So you might like someone's Smell one day and not the next.

Think about that!

That's about keeping people liking how you Smell.

That's about not just thinking you've got them and then dropping the ball by shifting your attention to the next project, but it's staying at it, refining and rebuilding, always producing the kind of pheromones of hygienic Leadership you want them to follow.

Since people can Smell fear and disgust on someone's sweat, it follows that they can also smell your manipulations.

You *must* have the Odor of Adore—not just to get adoration, but to give it. It's a mutual feedback loop of chemical receptivity. So, if you want to Lead, you must be Led.

No one can take your place, but you can lose it.

Every human has their own distinct Odor. Odor is like a fingerprint; you can't really fake it and no one can pretend to be you (Brian, 2010). You also can't hide or pretend you're somebody else. People will know. They will Smell you.

What you can do, however, is control your pheromone production through your intention.

I believe this because I have seen it and done it. I examined the concept through experimentation and observation, not double-blind studies and literature reviews.

This is *not* a scientifically proven fact, though it is being studied. However, like all scientific proving the studies follow behind the discoveries made through experience by people in the field.

It may not be a proven fact but it is a Brain Broad belief, and I suggest you buy it.

There's enough evidence for us to say it's plausible. And believing in plausibility makes it so.

If you think in terms of, "When I Adore people, when I stand on stage and Adore people, they Adore me back." I promise the Odor of your pheromones will be pungent with attractive chemical signalers.

Imagine yourself on stage, like in so many of my other examples. You're standing on the stage, looking out at your audience and deciding that you want to give them a gift.

I actually do this every time I take the microphone.

The questions I ask myself are, "What can I give these people today? What do these people need? What are they asking for? What are they responding to?" When I'm using all my senses to discover them, I am sending my Odor of Adore out into the crowd. I'm caring about them. And when they smell that, then they send their Odor of Adore back to me and I become their only focus. And because of the way pheromones hook the brain and reshape the attention of a person, even if I am on that stage with others, others who are not as skilled at the Odor of Adore, I am the only one the audience will see.

This is similar to when your six-year-old daughter is performing in a dance recital. You see only her and take pictures of only her; and though you are aware that the others are up there with her, your brain ignores them.

This tunnel vision of attention and perSEEing happens when we love, exclusively.

So you SEE, SMELL and HEAR only her, because you ADORE your six-year-old with your whole mind and body. And since she ADOREs you back, the attention-vibes are passing between you, connecting you, through the similarly tunnel-visioned crowd. Each parent is aware of only one particular child, unless they have twins.

So, since to be a GREAT Leader you must be heard when you speak, it follows that you must also be the center of focused ADORation when you share your life changing message. To accomplish this, be ADORing.

When others are in the limelight with you, Adore those others and invite them to Adore you back. Let your Odors mingle. This is how you grow into a powerful force, Led by You.

Gratitude grows and suddenly everyone is showering beautiful pheromones in your direction! You're being given a gift! That you must give back! And the feedback loops build, grow, and make room for more.

And that is how you "turn on" the pheromones of Adoration. You Adore *first!*

You must Adore first, because, as you now know, Odor all on its own is just a smell.

Chapter Five

SENSE FIVE in the SEVEN SENSES of LEADERSHIP

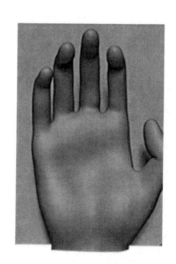

MYTH #9

Leaders are thinkers, not feelers!

In fact, Leaders are feelers who think. People with Leadership qualities are conscious of their emotions. They can control and mediate their behavioral responses to those emotions by shifting and adjusting themselves in accordance with the desired outcome. They use this skill to stay cognitively aware so that they can discover motivators in the people they Lead. This ability is called *Emotional Intelligence* and can be what differentiates a Leader from a follower (Goleman, Boyatzis, and McKee, 2013).

In some ways Feeling increases the ability to think. The Leader's brain is continuously screening sensory information, guided by emotions, to understand which task is worthy of attention. Thus, *emotionally intelligent* "Feelers who think" are fueling their ability to focus with emotion. In other words, when people with Leadership qualities get emotionally excited about a problem, the neurochemicals released in response to that excitement increases their observational efficiency. This helps them to accumulate more knowledge, notice anomalies, gather bits and pieces of data related to the challenge, as well as to engage in reflective reasoning to solve all problems encountered in the process of accomplishing said task. Excitement or passion, then, increases desire, which increases the ability to engage socially in a meaningful way; and this helps attract other people with common goals. These emotionally guided problem-solving skill experiences

Lead to a more sophisticated, more enriched neuronal system and enhanced physiological growth (Thompson, 1975).

Thus, it can be said that the brains of people with Leadership traits have practiced and attained the ability to become more fully informed by the emotion of sensory input: Feelers who think!

SENSE FIVE

FEELING YOUR WAY!

FEELing your way to the top requires a very acute awareness of your sense of Touch.

It's one of the earlier senses to come online when you're a baby in the womb. Your sense of Touch develops so that you can know to turn your head when there's pressure against the belly of your mother so as not get your little face squished (Fulkerson, 2013)! In fact, it's in that moment that the dance between one human being and another begins. The ability to move in concert with someone else's physiology is necessary if you want to be a successful Leader.

FEELing your way to the top is more than a metaphor. It's a reality.

In the physiology of our skin, we have many different aspects to Touch (Pastorino and Doyle-Portillo, 2012), (Doyle-Portillo and PASTORINO, 2005). For example, we *Feel* vibration, we *Feel* temperature, we *Feel* pressure, we *Feel* light touch, we *Feel* scratching, we *Feel* the stretching of our skin, we even *Feel* the proprioceptive information—which is when the joints are pushed together (Porter, 2013)—in order to get a sense of where our body is in this world (Porter, 2013).

In fact, proprioceptive information itself is so important that when it is disrupted people become "body blind" and unable to maneuver themselves in life without redirecting one of their other senses to take over the skill.

With all this attention to the body, it may seem like the sense of Touch is only about how things affect our bodies with no relationship to our brains, but in truth there is no division between the two—brain or body. They are all one thing, unless you break your neck.

Because, though Touch seems to happen in the body far away from your brain, the final experience actually takes place in your sensory neurons and frontal lobes with a lot of processing in between (Bernstein, 2010).

The sensation of Touch follows a long pathway of information passing— from the tips of your fingers or toes, or any external part where your skin meets with the environment—to nerve pathways that travel up the spinal cord and into the brain (Gates, 2010).

And here, in the brain, the experience of Touch becomes even more sophisticated and complex.

Understand why.

It is necessary for Touch to connect with action just as Smell must connect with emotion.

When we Smell danger we must immediately engage our other senses to "First Taste the pungency, then look, Hear, and *Feel* for the source of our concern." Nothing makes us collect our resources quicker than emotion.

So Smell gives us a *FEEL*ing, just as *FEEL*ing can cause us to *Smell* something fishy in our embracer's Touch.

When we *Feel* danger on our skin—as in the eyes on the back of our neck—we must be made immediately ready to act.

Thus Touch neurons and motor neurons must be connected.

Action isn't always the best response, though, so we must also be able to integrate and decide. During that whole integration and decision process, however, our muscles must remain ready to respond.

Additionally, for some Touch—like *burning hot*—action must be reflexive.

So *FEEL*ing your way to safety and success requires a cascade of responses and awarenesses integrated into a whole brain/body experience (Rosdahl and Kowalski, 2008).

Touch signals reach the brain where they are integrated by the parietal lobes as well as the cerebellum, which is an area of analysis (R. Carter, Aldridge, Page, and Parker, 2014). The basal ganglia gets involved so that you can learn *how* to move your body in response to the *FEEL*ing you just received (Dispenza, 2008)—like, "*Ouch! That stung! Move* away!" This area also helps to coordinate movement utilizing all the information being passed from your cumulative senses in order to perSEEv what to do next. Like, "That glass will miss the table, fall, and break. So move it a little more to the right." (McKenzie, 2013)

The actual sensory signal of *FEEL*ing happens in the sensory part of the sensorimotor strip, which runs from hemisphere to hemisphere over the middle of the brain (Baethmann, Go, and Unterberg, 2013).

This sensorimotor (Touch and movement) strip is represented by a homunculus (Kiernan and Rajakumar, 2013), which means that there's an area of the brain allocated for special neurons that are clustered together to fire when stimulated by signals passed to the brain from the touch sensors in your skin so that you can *Feel* and have the ability to responsively execute a movement (E. M. Marcus and Jacobson, 2012).

The homunculus looks like a brain-cell map of a distorted human being (Karczmar and Eccles, 2012). You have an area for the thumb, an area for the tongue, an area for the face; and they're all kind of misshapen in their representation within the brain because certain parts of our body need more sense of Touch than others (Gallace and Spence, 2014).

The tongue, for example, comprises a huge area of the homunculus with many, many neurons firing and reporting sensation (Sanes, Reh, and Harris, 2011). So in fact, you don't Feel the world from the outside.

You Feel it from the inside. All that information passes all the way through your body, up to your brain, and it's *your brain* that tells you what you Feel (Begley and Davidson, 2012), (M.D, 2010). This is an important reality.

There are two very relevant things to think about when it comes to *FEEL*ing your way to success, *FEEL*ing your way to the top, *FEEL*ing your way to becoming a Sensitive Leader that hones and refines their choices by utilizing their sense of Touch.

One: Touch is the way for you to connect with the external world, to know how much pressure you're putting on someone, to know when you're Touching them lightly, when you're Touching them deeply, when you're not Touching them at all (Mangal, 2013). Touch is actually the sense that enables you to concretely effect the things you perSEEv outside of yourself. Touch is how you manipulate the world that you live in, despite the fact that you experience it inside your brain.

Two: Touch is cocooned within moral, ethical, religious, and legal rules based on judgments that create a metamorphosis in your perSEption. Though this is true of all your senses, it is especially powerful in regards to Touch. Your beliefs will influence what you experience. This separation because of ideologies will happen despite your sense of Touch being the one sense you have that truly externalizes your experience and connects you with the world around you.

It is almost like a test—a Touch Test designed by nature to collect people into groups of agreed-upon distractions and separate the Leaders from the followers, the *FEEL*ers from the *Felt*.

Be a Leader. Focus and refine your ability to *FEEL*, and become aware of how you Touch others (Haggai, 2009). Take a moment to temporarily block the distractions of preconceived ideas, Sights, Sounds, Smells, and Tastes. Separate your senses so you can get your beliefs out of the way and *FEEL* what's really there.

If you do this you will be able to move with the flow and the energy of the people in your space. You will become one with those you Lead. You will not be tricked by the vibrations your brain is reading from a distance or the chemicals it's analyzing as they come in through the nose. You will actually know—through a controlled exchange of sensory feedback—exactly what it is that you are doing in relation to the other person.

True, you will have to put the beliefs back in, in order to verbalize and explain, in order to understand and share, and this will sculpt it into something new—cause you to make it up differently depending on the beliefs you embrace—but at least the raw material was unfiltered. Real.

Knowing what you *FEEL*, having clarity on why you want to Lead people, what it is that you want to Lead them to, and the way that you would define success if you got there, is extremely important.

Because the answers to these "Whys?" will decide the belief tools and stories you choose to work with and that will shape how everybody *Feels*.

||||||||||||||||||||||||||||||||||||||||||||| ▼ ▼ ▼ ||||||||||||||||||||||||||||||||||||||||||||||||||

LEADER: MAHATMA GANDHI 1869–1948, was a lawyer and spiritual Leader who advocated for the civil rights of Indians, both at home under British rule and in South Africa. After the outbreak of World War I, he moved from London and returned to India. He rejected his lawyer's suit and donned a loincloth and shawl, choosing to live the austere life of a spiritual Leader. He became known as "great soul" aka Mahatma (Allen, 2011).

However, in 1919 he mingled spirituality with politics by calling for peaceful protests in response to the Rowlatt Act, which allowed the British to imprison suspects without trial. His attempts at peaceful protestation were met with violence instead. The British killed approximately 400 people by opening fire on unarmed demonstrators (A. Carter, 1995).

Gandhi spent the next 29 years leading peaceful protests, living in and out of prison and fasting as a means of getting countrymen cooperation.

Gandhi led the Indian National Congress and advocated a policy of non-violence and non-cooperation to achieve home rule. In 1930, in one of his more notable adventures, Gandhi protested the Salt Acts—which prohibited Indians from collecting or selling salt—by walking in a loin cloth and shawl to the coastal town of Dandi (a 24-day trek) where he gathered a crowd. He then broke the law by making salt from evaporated seawater (Littel, 2006).

That year Gandhi and 60,000 Indians went to jail for similar acts.

Over the years Gandhi went in and out of prison, often accompanied by his wife, for acts of nonviolent noncompliance. After he launched the "Quit India" movement, meant to pressure The British into withdrawing from Indian Rule, he was again jailed. This time (1944) his wife died in his arms during their incarceration (Sherrow, 1994).

Gandhi wanted a unified India, but during independence negotiations of 1945, it became obvious he would not prevail and that there would be a partition of the subcontinent, along religious lines, creating two independent states Hindu (mostly Indian) and Muslim (mostly Pakistan).

Violence between the Hindus and Muslims erupted.

Gandhi went on another hunger strike to end the discord. However, his desire to unite the religious peoples caused hatred and feelings of betrayal by some Hindus. In 1948 Gandhi, now 78, left his home to pray and was shot at point blank range by a Muslim who first knelt at Mahatma's feet. Godse, the killer, was executed for committing such a violent act (Malgonkar, 2008).

It seems an unfitting end for a pacifist who preached non-violence and steadfastly stood for unity to be violently killed by anger and religiosity.

However, true and certain Leaders know their purpose and cannot help but live exemplary lives of purity and commitment. For Gandhi, this commitment was to non-violence and his belief in simple living.

Gandhi developed over the years and grew into his beliefs politically. He developed his viewpoint and took action once he had a clear vision. He wasn't born knowing it; he developed it in his years in South Africa. And because he took the time to find his purpose and then act upon it, he now represents hope for marginalized people throughout the world.

Gandhi died having fully lived the life of a LEADER.

And he lived the life he believed he must. Beliefs come first.

|||||||||||||||||||||||||||||||||||||||||||||| ▲ ▲ ▲ ||||||||||||||||||||||||||||||||||||||||||||||||

Martyrdom is a choice!

I want to explain the "belief-distortion effect" very thoroughly, even though I think by now you're starting to recognize how much your beliefs create and recreate, define and redefine, stop and Lead, to all the things in your experience. There is still something bigger to comprehend.

Emotional commitment to an idea changes a moment. It changes what you See, what you Taste, what you Smell, and what you Hear. It is especially strong when it comes to what you *Feel*. In fact, science has been able to ascertain which brain waves increase pain, and even that when a significant other gives sympathy, the evoked potential for pain is magnified greatly.

I love this hard science support for a phenomenon I have often observed: That the minute someone gives a person sympathy, that person will experience more pain—emotional or physical or both.

What that means in regards to Leadership Sensibilities is that to be a good Leader, you must be attentive to your people, empathetic with their causes, but *not* sympathetic to their pain, in any way that is going to amplify it (Cohn and Moran, 2011).

These fine lines that we walk upon are the definers of Leadership.

For example—in regards to group therapy—an understanding of these subtle differences can identify and/or design a Leader who Leads, moves people to a goal, and takes the members in the group away from their need for that group. Similarly, this understanding of subtleties and sympathetic reinforcement will highlight the Leader who Leads them nowhere, keeping them in place, adding to their pain, and reinforcing the problem to keep them needing the group, forever.

As you stand in front of people and say, "Come this way," it's important that you do it with the right sense of Touch, with the right amount of pressure, with the right amount of lightness, and with the right amount of freedom.

In the same way that we can increase someone's pain when we gather together to commiserate, we can also relieve their pain in the way we give them purpose and a mission in life, and focus them into the future built by their present moment.

You will have to *Feel* your way and discover your rightness, moment to moment, group to group.

It's not so much the sense of pressure, for example, that is good or bad. There's pressure when you hug somebody and feel the shape of their body pushing against yours; and if you love that person, you just experienced something warming to your soul and energizing.

But if you *do not* want to be hugged by someone and they force it upon you, you lose your freedom to choose, to enjoy, and to relax and breathe into the sensation. Thus the pressure feels like pain—it feels like imprisonment.

And a loss of freedom makes people want to escape.

You can't Lead people who are running away from you.

So, it isn't that there is a particular amount of pressure that can be given that is the perfect amount of pressure—it's the relationship and the belief that is instilled in the person before the pressure is applied. Working with anyone to emit change and encourage them to grow in a particular direction requires a certain amount of pressure, and it requires a certain amount of gentle Touch, tickling them forward. It also requires a grounded, open-armed invitation to come forward and follow. *FEEL*ing your way requires the ability to make a kind of temperature adjustment (Arwood and Kaulitz, 2007). When they *Feel* hot and deflated, they want coming close to you to *Feel* like coolness and energy. Conversely if they *Feel* cold and separated from other human beings, they may want to *Feel* warmed-up and connected by your presence.

> *"It's often just enough to be with someone. I don't need to touch them. Not even talk. A feeling passes between you both. You're not alone."*
>
> ~ Marilyn Monroe

*FEEL*ing your way requires *FEEL*ing, and filling, your audience's needs.

To be able to keep your focus on Leading by focusing on your followers and *FEEL*ing their presence while standing firmly in your own, it's necessary to, literally, become one big enormous being. You must extend your antennae of Touch receptors, open them to the invisible contact of opinion, and *Feel* your way to the top.

Take a minute when you *Feel* confused, or when you're trying to stand in your power, to shut down the distractions of all your other senses and simply *Feel* the people in your world. Become the grounding rod to their confused energy. In the same way that a lightning rod outside is meant to get the lightning to come to it, to go there, and keep everything else safe, you can keep your people safe by being the grounding rod for their attention. Stand in the space; do not be distracted by all the details, and ground your energy. They will follow (Riggio, Chaleff, and Lipman-Blumen, 2008). In that way you will bring the ability to *Feel* them to you without having to reach across the space and invade their bodies.

Touching others—even figuratively—requires being fully in yourself and then reaching across by opening up to others and drawing them in.

So, *Feel* your way to the top. Draw people in.

Give them something to hope for, to work for, and to focus on; and everybody's pain reduces and goes away. It's called the Pain Gate Theory (D. Marcus, 2009), (Greenstein and Greenstein, 2007). When extended to this concept, it means: You can't focus on your pain when you are focused on your goal. This is because one focus pushes out the other.

So share your pain-free vision of the moment.

That's the greatest gift a Leader can give to others and to him or herself.

A *FEEL*ing of exuberance and a zest for life.

Give the hugeness of this gift while maintaining your attention to the details.

There's a neat aspect to Touch that exemplifies your astute ability to detect minute details and differences. It's the ability to recognize vibration.

Think of your fingers. They have the ability to ascertain whether a weave has big squares in it or some little squares in it, or if it's consistent (Achterberg, 1994). You can run your finger across any kind of textural surface, and you're able to sort of see it with your mind's eye (Hunter, 2012). Without looking you can envision the shapes and sizes, know the roughness and the softness, and understand the relevance and the irrelevance of everything you Touch (McConnell, 1983).

Where that comes in for Leaders is that a Leader's sense of Touch must have a refined ability to ascertain consistencies and inconsistencies in characters. A Leader must be able to identify the people that are being smooth from the ones that are a little bit roughly textured in their approach to life (Hook, 2009).

You should want this skill.

You should want this sensational skill, fine-tuned and made instinctive. Great Leaders can *Feel* the people who are resisting them and not *Feel* pulled on, or shifted from, their place as a grounding rod. Great Leaders understand that often the people who are resisting the position of follower are people of texture and character with lots to offer—not necessarily the enemy (Finzel, 2012).

Too many Leaders misread resistance as a problem, where instead, I would suggest you see it as a learning opportunity to exercise your commitment.

Different perspectives do not subtract; they add enrichment.

The more that you have to consider the *FEEL*ings of the people you Lead and their natural resistance to blindly following, the more you will have to learn to Lead. Then, like exercising the stretch receptors in the skin (Brodal, 2016), (Tresilian, 2012), their resistance to being pulled and pushed makes it so that the more they resist the more you grow and become sophisticated and capable (Kenshalo, 2012).

Your resisters and your followers—all your people are your gift.

Lead them with care.

Feel your way to the top so that they can follow suit and *Feel* their way there as well.

The best Leaders, Leaders like you, have followers who pass them on the mountain, become a new force, and make your dreams come true.

Chapter Six

SENSE SIX in the SEVEN SENSES of LEADERSHIP

MYTH #10

All Leaders are adrenalin junkies addicted to their own success.

Generally speaking Leaders are addicted to Leading; if that also includes looking and sounding like a social and financial success, even better.

When people are out of balance they seek relief. When people are asked to go against their natural style, they fall out of balance. Leaders are generally people who feel more comfortable making decisions than following them, so in this way they need a role of authority. Hence Leaders are addicted to Leading.

However, not all Leaders achieve balance and comfort simply by taking the Lead. Some do it by focusing on work, some by riding roughshod over their employees, and some by snorting cocaine. When nonflexible Leaders feel their authority threatened, they can fall out of balance. This puts them at risk of holding too tightly to the reigns. And holding to the reigns of their followers makes them a marionette puppeteer, not a Leader.

It isn't a myth to say that some Leaders are adrenalin junkies backing themselves up against deadlines to create a panic response in the brain. Some Leaders do, do that. However, for the adrenalin-seeking Leader using panic for focus, the myth is that adrenaline is a good tool for optimal problem solving.

Those who have seen the movie classic *Pulp Fiction* likely remember the scene in which John Travolta's character slammed a needle full of adrenalin into a seemingly dead heroin-overdosed-mobster's wife in the hopes of saving her life. It worked and she sat bolt upright from dead to ... well... not dead. Though, admittedly, she still looked like death warmed over; she seemed to no longer be at risk (Tarantino, 1994).

This is a Hollywood version of a no longer used approach and, of course, they took some liberties; but in fact it is possible to have an overdose victim receive an intercardiac injection of Epinephrine (aka Adrenalin which speeds the beat and strengthens the power of the heart's contractions) (Stolk, U'Prichard, and Fuxe, 1988) accompanied by Atropine (Acetylecholine antagonist that increases heart rate and reduces salivation) (Walsh and Schwartz-Bloom, 2004) and Narcan (an opioid antagonist that counters the effects of opioid overdose like heroine or morphine) (Rhoads 2014) and sit "bolt upright."

It's not the usual method, nor the likeliest response, and in general one would want to medicate slowly so as not to send the victim into withdrawal ...but it could and has happened almost like it did in the movie.

And that is often the situation behind myth formation. A story, whether told or portrayed, capitalizes on a crumb of truth and then expands that into something misleading. In fact, this type of manipulation for personal and company gain is also the truth in marketing and politics, but let's stay out of that rabbit hole.

Being misled by wishful thinking married with misinformation can have dire consequences. Being afflicted with *Adrenaline Love* is a good example because a lot of propaganda supports that type of addiction. A movie scene like this one in *Pulp Fiction* can leave the lasting impression that adrenaline is good for the heart and possibly lifesaving. In general, this is opposite of the truth.

Being part of the "Thinkers who Feel" crowd generally translates into a strong affection for cognitive clarity. Though adrenaline can be a focus helpmate by increasing a sluggish heart rate, repeatedly flooding one's system with adrenaline has some serious health repercussions. Let's start by explaining what adrenaline is.

Adrenaline is a hormone produced in the medulla of the adrenal glands from where it is released into the bloodstream (D. K. E. Carter and Seifert, 2012). It has many different actions depending on the type of cells it is acting upon. Adrenaline has been called the *"Fight or Flight"* hormone as its release is only increased at times of acute stress (Wright, 2000), (Hall and Halliday, 1998). However, it can more accurately be termed a motivational (do it IMMEDIATELY!) drug that allocates extra resources and gives you the means to do it IMMEDIATELY! It is an addictive neurochemical dump that gives you an extra burst of energy to handle a crisis (Goldstein, 2008).

When something unexpected happens that the brain and its magnificent system of hormones perSEEves as threatening your body, it dumps several hormone shots of super fuel into your blood stream (Gray, 1987). For the next few minutes you're going to be super charged to deal with the situation IMMEDIATELY! The triggering event, this something unexpected, can be coming from the outside environment OR the inside.

One example is when chemical shifts in the brain unexpectedly release an intense memory (Sanchez, 2008). Whether this was cued by an internally driven change in blood sugar or an externally driven BANG that your brain may have associated with gunfire, in some ways you are at the mercy of your unconscious brain. This is because often even the externally driven events are imperceptible to our conscious mind. For example, a minute smell or peripheral shadow is enough to trigger the memory of that day your boyfriend asked you to marry him. Then, at the point when the smell or peripheral shadow cues your brain, it will use its memory files and cause you to react both internally and externally, in a similar neurochemical fashion to the day it is remembering (Damasio, 1999). In other words you will FEEL according to your brain's memory patterns.

Your reaction will be different than someone who has a different association to that smell or sound because your reaction comes from your own individualized beliefs built upon experience and exposure to ideas. You have been building that associative-brain-filing system your entire life. This high excitement response that is so famously known as the "flight or fight" reaction of our brains and bodies moves so fast that it arrives before you can even have a conscious thought (James, 2007). And that is why we often behave in ways we ourselves do not understand. Because the memory never even surfaced into our awareness before the chemicals were released. So, good actions, bad actions, happy feelings, sad feelings, in fact all reactions, both seen and unseen, are mingled together and filtered through a network of past experiences and associated beliefs (Elsner and Farrands, 2012).

What does that have to do with adrenaline junkie Leaders and their Leadership Sensibilities? EVERYTHING!

Like any drug, adrenaline can benefit us when released in the correct moment for an appropriate purpose. Like any psycho-stimulant, adrenaline is addictive (Forest and Light, 1999). Also like any psycho-stimulant, our brains and bodies get used to the dosage and down regulate receptors, while up regulating the desire. Thus, the addict is born. He or she begins craving more, chasing the proverbial carrot on a stick, forever eluded but always hoping to get the same focused brain buzz as that *first time effect*.

WARNING: repeatedly flooding one's system with adrenaline causes some serious health challenges (Bryant and Knights, 2011), (Rassool, 2011).

Understand that your body is a contained system. That means when you get an adrenaline dump, the chemicals released into you system don't just magically vanish. They stay within your blood affecting your nervous system, perceptions, and physiology until they are reabsorbed back into the system and out into the trash. While adrenaline can be introduced quickly, it's going to take time to be reabsorbed, broken down and eliminated (Hoffman, 2013).

If you want to be a great Leader, or even a healthy follower, STOP shooting up and injecting your body from within: When adrenaline is released in response to perceived danger, it gives you a burst of power and speed (Williams and Denney, 2010).

But it also distorts time, making it seem as if you are traveling in slow motion. It warps vision and depth perception, making things seem bigger and closer than they are as well as resulting in tunnel focus that prevents you from factoring in things from outside of your attention. It closes down hearing and muffles or eliminates the sounds of even your own screams. Strength and speed increases in the gross motor system like legs and arms; but the fine motor system, which is much more important in today's world for operating the technology you have on hand, is negatively affected. So you lose dexterity and begin to tremble just when you need to be precise and steady. Adrenaline can shut down or partly close the brain's sensory connection to body sensations, and with that the ability to feel pain.

These last two particular effects can leave you looking very un-Leader-like while you drop your water glass, mess up your power point, trip and bump into the lectern, oblivious to the pain sensations that should be warning you to stand your ground and not fall off the stage. Fortunately, and unfortunately, you will also likely experience enough cognitive distortion that you remember yourself as having done great, even if you weren't received well at all. This adrenalin-driven cognitive distortion is a good reason for feedback forms that anonymously share audience opinion.

Unless the people you wish to Lead are residents in an insane asylum, you may want to avoid dosing yourself with the distortions of adrenalin-assisted delusions of grandeur.

The point is: *If you are consistently in this state you may be wrong about everything you think you know about yourself.*

So, yes, your heart will beat faster from adrenalin. But for many more reasons than accurate metacognition, consistently using it to fuel your decisions is a *very bad idea!*

Slightly broken Leaders are the ones who prioritize their area of interest to such a degree that every other aspect of their life falls apart. This dichotomy between comfort and discomfort is extremely stressful and leads to huge psychological health issues. In order to stand up for your mission, being balanced everywhere in your life is paramount. Otherwise you can't stand up for what you stand for (Cooper, 2012).

Additionally, in this technological time, being self-made has been given a new connotation. Self-promoting is available globally for little to no fee via the Internet, so many self-made Leaders are their own publicity agent.

Interestingly, self-promoters often come to believe their own press, even though they are the ones who wrote it. This possibly delusional belief is facilitated by cloud-based analytics and coerces you via your computers and smart phones. Since Facebook, Google, and the like can now target in a way that shows you only the world you want to see, it is easy to become convinced that the lie you see on your screen is the whole truth and nothing but the truth, so help you Google.

If your screen world displays you as a super star, then awesome for you; but don't be disappointed if nobody recognizes you at the grocery store because their computer screen is displaying a different story.

The new analytics do exactly that; they show us our own interests and reduce the likelihood of seeing each other's concerns. In some ways this is like a computer-driven form of globally created autism.

So how do self-made self-promoting thought Leaders avoid becoming addicted to their own self image and continue to grow?

What do you do if you have this habit?

Interrupt the cycle.

Even if you are an adrenaline junkie who thrives on the excitement of edgy living, practice the art of *"every other time."*

In other words, when you want to placate your own self vision and scare yourself into a good high, do something else, *every other time.*

You may think this is unimportant because you may have heard that something called *eustress* is good for the brain and/or body. But even *eustress*, often associated with high-energy excitement related to activities like Xtreme sports, can turn into *distress*. Stress is stress when it becomes chronic and harmful to your overall health (Lovallo, 2015).

So, instead of moving to quick decisions when overloaded with a burgeoning schedule, take a quick ten-minute walk on the treadmill first, *every other time* (Lehrer, Woolfolk, and Sime, 2007).

This pattern interrupt could be key to redirecting your body's stress response. But even *"every other time"* is a systematic foreseeable pattern that can result in behavioral addiction. So organize your office or work area and do the pattern-interrupt every other, other time, every little once in a while. Keep changing the pattern (Ascher and Levounis, 2015).

Breathe in a deep steady rhythm while looking for gentler solutions and use movement. Breathing and moving both change the flow of your body's chemistry. Your world may be brimming with excitement and opportunities for success, but in this case, too much of a good thing can be bad. Mental and physical fluidity, relaxation, and contentment are crucial to maintaining your role as a healthy vibrant Leader (Covey, 1999).

Focus your attention on what is happening in the present moment. **Don't** make a story out of what you SEE that will bring up negative emotions like fear, hurt, anger, etc. **Do** make a story if it affirms the positive. If you already FEEL angry, hurt, or annoyed, don't overlay meaning onto it. If you FEEL joyful make *that* important. Go for a walk. Step away, even if the best excuse you can manage is a trip to the bathroom. Uncontrolled, reactive negative emotion, especially PANIC is NEVER a good idea (Freeman, 2007).

Especially for a Leader.

Unless your followers want to run around in a state of hysteria in order to create a contagious panic in the asylum.

Here is the real secret to Leadership Sensibility: Purposely choose words and actions that benefit others. The more you consciously choose actions and words that benefit others, the further your prefrontal cortex (associated with creative thought and executive function) develops with thoughts of love and compassion for yourself and others (B. L. Miller and Cummings, 2007). This releases oxytocin (the love hormone), motivates you into taking action, and feeds the positive cycle (Ostafin, Robinson, and Meier, 2015).

These motivated actions will be special because they will be inclusive and intended to benefit others, as well as yourself.

Think of solving your adrenaline addiction as similar to gaining any new ability through practice, self-education, and reflection. That is how you build good habit systems with a twist. Do it different! Newness is both healthy and a little stressful.

Brains rewire for new possibilities each time a person steps in the direction of new solutions (O'Connor, 2015). That positive tone offers a gateway into multiple possibilities for high-performing minds. So add variety and increase your mental flexibility. You will enjoy many health benefits (Marques, 2014).

This way, as long as you don't make variety a *"must or should"* and force yourself back into the box of fear, you can have your adrenalin cake and eat it too.

WARNING: don't just shift addictions.

Some out-of-balance, would-be Leaders turn to stimulants. This is because stimulants, like cocaine, cause the brain to shift to an outward focus (Koob, Arends, and Moal, 2014). This quickly achieved ability to see all the possibilities is reminiscent of the movie *Limitless* wherein the characters can take a pill that makes them able to compute and comprehend all cause-and-effect, problem-related solutions at lightning speed.

The desire for this type of immediately accessed super-human brain is itself addictive. However, overuse of stimulants, prescribed or black market, particularly cocaine, can make you see more than real-life possibilities. Stimulants can also make you see pretend people. This is because overuse of stimulants like cocaine can lead to paranoid schizophrenia (Sachdev and Keshavan, 2010). Cocaine is a serotonin-norepinephrine-dopamine reuptake inhibitor, also known as a triple reuptake inhibitor (Baumeister and Bushman, 2013). Let's focus on the dopamine piece.

Reuptake inhibitor means that the breakdown of dopamine is inhibited so it stays available for use longer. Dopamine is a natural stimulant (Davis and Neuropsychopharmacology, 2002). It's one of our brain's super feel-good transmitters, and most motivated people are producing lots of it. Some folks call it "the motivational hormone" (Dunnett, Bentivoglio, Björklund, and Hökfelt, 2004).

Since dopamine is a natural stimulant, it makes sense that when there isn't enough of it we can end up depressed, slow thinking, slow moving and, if the lack of dopamine continues, be plagued by symptoms of Parkinson's (Duvoisin and Sage, 2001).

The connection between schizophrenia and Parkinson's is that when the brain produces too little dopamine, a diagnosis of Parkinson's is one of the possible results. However, with too much dopamine, schizophrenia is the likely label (Kaufman, 2007). This was aptly portrayed in the movie *Awakenings* with Robin Williams who portrayed Oliver Sacks, the doctor who originally discovered this Parkinson's/Schizophrenia connection. Ironically, Robin Williams killed himself partially as a result of his own newly discovered Parkinson's-related depression (Marshall, 1991). Just as the movie showed us, often the drugs used to help schizophrenics induce Parkinson's symptoms. Similarly, people who use cocaine long enough to damage their serotonin-norepinephrine-dopaminergic system often end up with cocaine-induced schizophrenia.

If you are feeling the pressure mount and considering cocaine in order to get more done, be wary. You just may end up leading whole companies that nobody else can see.

And even if you don't get schizophrenia, you still might have a heart attack.

Dopamine is *super addictive,* and if you are revving your system and hyper focusing on one area of interest, you are likely running on dopamine. High performers like Robin Williams who exhaust their dopaminergic system fit the profile for Parkinson's and depression (Herbert, 2014).

Hyper focusing leads to health risks. Balance and cross-discipline learning are the key successful Leadership traits.

Alzheimer's is another potential downside to a hyper-focused way of being. If you look at the data the best Alzheimer's preventative life style choice is to vary your interests and intellectual endeavors (Lu and Bludau, 2011).

Unfortunately it is common to discover that your favorite thought Leader has no tolerance for conversation outside their narrow field of interest. I believe this is because the definition of success has not been widened to include personal relaxation and eclectic skill acquisitioning. This is a problem for many Leaders, both now and in their future.

There are many bosses who overwork their employees because they themselves are driven. They find what they do so darn interesting they can't imagine that others don't feel the same way.

I am a neurofeedback professional helping people to interrupt brain wave feedback loops that have gotten stuck firing in a maladaptive way. One of the things I see when looking at hyper-focused obsessive-compulsive behavior is synchronized fast firing near the area correlated with the brain's anterior cingulate (Bourne, Eckhardt, Sheth, and Eskandar, 2012). I can use my therapy to reduce the amplitude of that fast firing activity and improve the story for these people. But a change in behavior will do it as well.

The point is, who you are changes what you do and what you do changes who you are, and some of these choices are things you can control.

Let's go back to the flight or fight response of your sympathetic nervous system.

Since dopamine is released during fear, adrenalin is obviously not the only fear hormone. In fact, cortisol is a slower acting hormone released immediately after an adrenalin dump and is a part of the fear response. It is intended to reset the system (Jarvis and Watts, 2012). You have likely heard about it on the news or in commercials, especially if you are someone with too much tummy weight, because excess cortisol in the system causes people to keep their belly fat (Talbott and Kraemer, 2007), and some drug marketers have capitalized on that fact.

Cortisol is slower to release and slower to leave the system than adrenalin. Its effects are wide reaching. This is a good thing in emergencies.

However, chronic release of cortisol creates a system that gets stuck in a loop and doesn't know when to turn itself off.

Adrenaline and cortisol, which are released to help you cope with a critical incident or stressful event, continue to build up in the body, sometimes reaching toxic levels (Colbert, 2003). At this point almost all of your major organs and systems are at great risk for disease, including the heart, digestive system, and brain.

When you recognize that the neurochemical cascade of your body's stress response is not turning off due to the harmful effects of chronic stress, it's not too late to make the necessary changes and prevent overwhelming illness.

Start by NOT doing mental gymnastics with scientific facts to shore up and excuse your internally driven neurochemical addiction.

Instead duck and weave, flex and stretch, and choose and re-choose in a state of calm. Value composure.

One of the problems in getting Leaders who like adrenalin to use mental Aikido instead of going head-to-head when problem solving is the advertised positives of adrenaline to the body. These misunderstood truths are misleading.

For, though it is true that exercise-led adrenaline release may contribute to the feeling of invincibility that a Leader needs in order to trust his fast decision-making skills without the same degree of negative after-effects and destruction as that created by panic and pressure, this type of adrenalin release has different adaptations by the body's network of organs and cells. Don't trick yourself into getting your "hit" the easy way by choosing "scared" and then equating it to the same thing as exercise-driven adrenaline with all its health advantages. The panic of pressure is NEVER beneficial (Freeman, 2007).

A good question at this point might be: *Is the Leader's brain actually just about hormones? And can the addiction loops be that easily interrupted?*

It is a good question: And the answer is no, and the answer is yes.

Since all behavior and even the energy with which we signal others is reflected in our hormones, the answer must be "yes," the Leader's brain is all about hormones.

Fact is, like The Butterfly Effect (mathematician Edward Lorenz's metaphor for chaos theory), in the universe of our individual selves you can't affect any system without in some way impacting another. So hormones are a good beginning place from which to recreate, and that Leads us to the second part of the question. Yes, Leaders can interrupt the loop at any point in its cycle. As for easy, well, that depends on the Leader, their hormones, their leanings for panic and addiction, their willingness and motivation to change, all of which are hormonally driven.

So let me motivate you to change!

Adrenaline causes a rise in blood pressure. It causes some muscles to clench unconsciously resulting in migraines and muscle aches while simultaneously causing other muscles to relax resulting in strange areas of weakness (Saito, 1988). Respiration becomes faster and can over-oxygenate your system so much so that you freeze into panic and your hands feel like huge clenched lobster claws that are beyond your control (Buijs and Swaab, 2013). And if that isn't reason enough, understand that bladder and bowel release are common and part of why most speakers need a preshow (hopefully not "in show") bathroom visit. And the more you do this the more it becomes how you operate.

Making a habit of juicing yourself with adrenaline in order to get things done strongly recreates the body you live in.

Not only are you affected during the hormonal release but there are serious after-effects:

- Nausea.

- Hypomania (during the cool-down period and as adrenaline is "digested" by our refuse system, some people get the jitters, others fidget and pace, others rapidly babble, some yell and shout, and some people do them all).

- Body aches.

- A total crash into complete exhaustion leaving the system vulnerable to viruses and bacteria.

- An opposite restless sleeplessness accompanied by bad or weird vivid dreaming.

- Horniness (possible reason why so many of the adrenaline Leaders are also infamously promiscuous and/or hypersexual).

- Erection and ejaculation can also be a byproduct (especially if the adrenaline is related to an act of violence) and though more common in men, women may also experience changes like erect nipples or sexual release (Greenfield and Sternbach, 1972).

All these things could be counterproductive, to say the least, if you're on stage delivering an inspirational message to your followers.

As is made obvious by the last statement, adrenaline rushes can feel positive in nature and are part of what makes things fun for many (e.g., extreme sports) (Constantini and Hackney, 2013). However, the person who abuses this magnificent system to get work done is no longer fueling decisions with their rational mind.

Executive functions shut down during an adrenalin dump, and if you stay in this state for too long and you don't have a well-rehearsed preexisting strategy that your body can perform without its "thinking" brain, you run the risk of freezing altogether. Thus using fear limits creativity and keeps you in the box of your own thinking. Fear is the enemy of Leadership (Bogue, 1985).

A happy, passionate, goal-oriented behavioral system is the bedrock of success. Creative thought is your vehicle for greatness because creative thought takes you beyond the boundaries of previous experience.

Fortunately, you can drop your cortisol levels simply by standing in a control stance (legs apart, arms outspread) for two minutes. Phew! That was easy.

A simple purposeful move like this sets you up for a whole different chemical bath, more beneficial than any kind of adrenalin rush.

In order to grow strong you must learn how to turn off your body's stress response so that it doesn't send excessive amounts of adrenaline and cortisol coursing through the bloodstream. In addition to power poses, regular exercise, healthy relationships, meditation, and cutting back on alcohol consumption are at least four ways to reduce the impact of stress on the body (Davidson, 2001).

I use biofeedback for the brain to interrupt the cycle of adrenalin, dopamine addiction, serotonin syndrome, and other hormone imbalances because healthy Leadership Sensibilities require a healthy balance of brain waves. And because I just happen to have it in my home.

(For a complete description of neurofeedback, commonly called biofeedback for the brain, see the seventh sense.)

SENSE SIX

EQUALIBRIUM

Being Balanced requires a sense of EQUALity or EQUALibrium. Unlike most people's concept of the sixth sense, your Leadership Sensibilities' sixth sense is a sense of Balance.

For our purposes EQUALibrioception is a sense of Balance, and fairness.

In fact, according to Wikipedia, Balance is one of the physiological senses.

I remember when I was learning neuroanatomy, some of the questions that were being investigated were: "Should Balance be considered the sixth sense?" and "Are there more than five senses?" and "If so, what is the definition of a sense and how do we rewrite it to include everything?"

Unfortunately, this openness to scientific evolution unlocked the gates of insanity letting in arguments for everybody's favorite brain talent to become a dedicated sense. The debates ensued with very little decision-making following suit.

So the fear mongering began and worries of sense dilution were voiced using exaggerated examples like: "Before you know it, we'll be writing books on 'the sense of blinking your eyes.'"

Sometimes people can be silly, especially when they lack Leadership and a sense of EQUALibrium.

At this point in our evolution the uncertainty remains and many neurologists identify nine senses while some stretch the envelope all the way to twenty-one.

We will escape this debate by being definitive and identifying only Seven Senses of Leadership.

Now, for our purposes, I agree with Wikipedia. Balance is a sense. So let's discuss it.

Our sixth of seven senses, EQUALibrium is the sense of being and behaving with Balance. EQUALity isn't always sameness. EQUALlibrium understands how to integrate, segregate, blend, and decide what comes next.

Balanced decisions are done with kindness, and kindness sometimes looks like saying "no." In fact, knowing how to deliver bad news with a sense of equanimity is a much-needed Leadership skill, necessary for retaining one's Leadership EQUALibrium (Junarso, 2009),(Kucia and Gravett, 2014).

Great Leaders are good at "no" but they are also good at "yes."

EQUALibrium for Leaders, as it turns out, happens in a state of clarity that is derived from focus that is aimed at achievement—for all.

IIIIIIIIIIIIIIIIIIIIIIIIIIIIIIIIIIIIIIIIIIIII   IIIIIIIIIIIIIIIIIIIIIIIIIIIIIIIIIIIIIIIIIIIIIIIIII

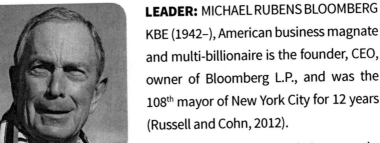

LEADER: MICHAEL RUBENS BLOOMBERG KBE (1942–), American business magnate and multi-billionaire is the founder, CEO, owner of Bloomberg L.P., and was the 108th mayor of New York City for 12 years (Russell and Cohn, 2012).

Bloomberg was elected just weeks following the September 11 terrorist attacks on the trade towers. Due to his wealth he was able to run for this office without bending to lobby groups or vested interests. It is reported that he spent 650 million dollars of his own money on New York City during his time as mayor. He also gave up the yearly 2.7 million-dollar salary and went out-of-pocket on all expenses related to traveling with staff and security (*Arts Management*, 1999).

Bloomberg's views are clearly stated and backed by millions of dollars. He works to shape legislation and has committed 600 million to anti-tobacco efforts globally as well as millions more to road safety efforts in Brazil, Vietnam, and Egypt. Presently he has been reported as a man trying to create a coalition of Mayors Making a Difference countrywide.

In this much abbreviated presentation of a very accomplished Leader it can be said, Bloomberg knows what he wants and does it.

||||||||||||||||||||||||||||||||||||||||||||||| ▲ ▲ ▲ |||||||||||||||||||||||||||||||||||||||||||||||||||

LEADER know thyself!

When you think about Balance itself, when you understand the neuroanatomy of our EQUALibrium processing, it almost feels as if Balance could be put under the umbrella sense of HEREing.

EQUALibrium FEELs like, "Be, HEAR, Now" because the vestibular system, the organ of Balance, is made up of three fluid-filled canals in various parts of the ear itself.

There are little semicircular canals located in the cochlea, which is a part of the inner ear. Their purpose is to guide your Balance (Noyd, Krueger, and Hill, 2016). If you want to imagine what it's like, think of that leveling tool you or your construction worker uses. You know; the one with the little bubble of air in the center. You lay it down and look at the little bubble of air inside that fluid-filled tube, and you look to see if it's in the center; and if it's in the center, the leveling tool is telling you that you have a nice, level floor or countertop or whatever it is you are attempting to Balance.

It's that simple. With this sweet little bubble of air, this bubble of nothing, you've found a sense of Balance for this aspect of your construction project.

People with their little semicircular canals located in the cochlea work in much the same way. We have fluid sloshing around and we achieve Balance from the way our inner ear is signaling us (Clark, 2005),(Nomura, 2013).

Of course, like all the senses there are other aspects to Balance: other parts of the brain that can interpret whether we're leaning right or leaning left in order to interject a state of EQUALibrium.

Fortunately, we can use these other parts to help ourselves if those leveling tools of the cochlea have been challenged and are no longer signaling us correctly (Heyning and Punte, 2010).

Like all the senses, we have enough processing redundancy to work with our strengths and educate our weaknesses.

I remember reading a book by the famous clinical neurologist Oliver Sacks (as mentioned, he is the doctor Robin Williams played in the movie *Awakenings*) called *The Man Who Mistook His Wife for a Hat* (Marshall, 1991).

In this collection of unusual case studies, there is a story about an older gentleman who had a problem with his Balance. He had difficulty moving forward and leaned to the left. So he and Oliver Sacks created a leveler attached awkwardly to his glasses. Before perfecting the leveler, they attempted to affix something called a *plumb line*. In case you don't know what a plumb line is, let me describe one you may have used. If you were trying to set your wallpaper correctly, straight up and down on the wall, you might take a bolt, and tie it to a string and tape it on the wall. Then you'd see how straight it falls and you'd line up the edges of your wallpaper to match the string. The bolt works much like the bubble did so that gravity can guide the leveling and you won't be fooled by the imperfect lines that exist in the world around you.

People follow the stimulus of the things they see and a plumb line, like a good Leader, helps keep you on track (*Life Stories of Authentic Leaders in Higher Education Administration*, 2007).

Thus, a plumb line is something that plays that role of guiding one into a state of Balance. You let gravity pull the heavy-weighted object straight down so that you can get a sense of what straight up and down actually looks like.

Plumb lines are a fantastic tool. Because straight up and down isn't as easy to detect as you might think. Illusions happen. False ideas and attractions abound, misinforming people and wreaking havoc on independent thought.

We look at the world around us and we get tricked. We get tricked by the change in the landscape, tricked by the leaning of a building, tricked by all the different things that are around us; and we lose our sense of what's up and what's down, what's real and what's imagined, what's kind and what's cruel.

Our realities are morphed by our senses so it's important to find a way to stay in control of what we perSEEv if we don't want to become just another member of *The Lost Leading the Lost*. Having healthy Leadership Sensibilities requires that a sense of reality be mixed into and blended nicely with that sense of EQUALibrium.

Okay, so here we are, easily fooled. We need a plumb line or a leveling tool. The older gentleman I was telling you about created a leveler for himself. His brain had stopped operating in the way that it should—his Parkinson's had damaged the communication pathways from the cochlea—and so he wasn't able to achieve a sense of upright Balance. He was unable to walk forward in a straight line and leaned many degrees to the left without realizing it. Once video taped and made aware of his tilt, he solved the problem by coming up with the idea of a leveler. Oliver Sacks helped him fashion it. And the leveler taught his brain how to compensate for his missing sensory information. Isn't that just brilliant!?

This man is a Leader. He Led himself and his doctor. I read about and remembered it. Thus—when my stroke caused disabling vertigo—he led me to Lead myself with a similar solution. (I used neurofeedback—which I will go into in the next chapter—and the wall against my skin to reorganize my sense of EQUALibrium.)

He Led himself, his doctor, and me; and now, because I am sharing the story with you, you are also being Led. You are being Led to understand that even a degenerating brain condition does not have to be accepted as fated and forever.

In some cases all it takes to be a Leader is the refusal to fall apart.

So this man, this Leader of self, designed his own solution and re-educated his EQUALibrium. He used the glasses plumb line and then the leveler to straighten out his own crooked demeanor. He looked at it, this string with a weight on the bottom, that was always straight up and down and always just in front of him, and he would try to walk keeping the string aligned with his nose. He was able to move forward because he was following his string. However, the string was swinging too close to his nose so they redesigned it with a long arm from the bridge of the nose attached to two horizontal levelers. This was bulky but effective. He stared at the horizontal arms as he walked, and if the bubbles in the leveler veered over towards one eye or the other, he knew that he was leaning, so he straightened up.

Eventually the effort this took became second nature and he walked upright with ease.

And this is how he retrained his visual cortex to take over the function of his inner ears Balance system.

Interestingly, using your visual cortex to maintain Balance and mobility is commonly taught (Champney, 2015). That is what dancers do when they "spot the wall" as they spin, and what sea-sick boaters do when they "stare at the horizon" to quell the nausea. It is what people with body blindness do when they can't stand because they can't feel their body. So instead, they walk with their eyes, looking at their legs. Thus they perSEEv their body into being through an alternative sense. Their eyes remove the blindness, bring their body into existence, and hence under their control. Even though all of these things were already known, none of this man's doctors thought of the plumb line or the leveler—not even Oliver Sacks. That is understandable. They were distracted by their beliefs.

Sometimes EQUALibrium is better achieved by people dealing with real problems in the real world, rather than the people educated into distraction, by the teachings within the specialized area of their particular expertise.

And that is an important aside, because real world Balance is the goal we want to get.

There are other brain-related aspects to Balance of course, but this book really isn't about you learning exactly how the brain functions and neither is this chapter. It's about the Balance of how we treat each other and how we Lead. It's about EQUALibrium.

There's a necessary kind of push-pull that happens in Leadership, in saying, "You can work harder," to somebody, or, "Love who you are and appreciate where you're at."

You want to push people to be the best they can be. While at the same time you want to pull them as a Leader to love themselves, which is another form of being the best that they can be; and if you don't apply the right amount of pressure, you'll fall down as a Leader and lose your Balance.

The Leader who pushes too hard, who is always cracking the whip on their people, that Leader may get results as far as what they see; but what'll happen is the people who are having the whip cracked on them will start to talk amongst themselves. They'll start to complain and compare notes, and though they may give the Leader the face of compliance and agreement, they will be preparing a mutiny. And then, they'll go find another Leader to follow, never having recognized the gains they may have gotten, because their focus was on the whip.

Pushing too hard just creates factions of disagreement amongst your tribe. Pulling too hard has a similar effect because if you're pulling and pulling and pulling, the exertion that is applied shows on your face. Your need to have them come close and follow becomes a sense of desperation, and people can see and feel that.

A true Leader is able to push and pull with the right amount of pressure, the right amount of switching (Kouzes and Posner, 2012). So think of that as the right and the left of Balance. If you veer too far to the right, you topple over and fall on the right side of your head; and if you veer too far to the left, you topple over and fall on the left side of your head. You want to walk a straight line between push and pull, and in doing that you will be able to stand your ground and say, "Come with me," while at the same time factoring in their difference, their landscape, their chaos.

Sometimes you must push. Some people don't like to be pulled but are in a state of inertia so they need a little push! If you are worried that you can't be a Leader because you are averse to pushing, what then?

Use a different Leadership Sense.

You can find another way to exert force, like using Vision to gain Balance.

Sometimes just turning your attention away will reverse your magnetism and push people into your particular playground. So, if you are averse to pushing, just *stop*, and turn your back. This is not a rejection. It's a vacuum builder that uses the propulsion created by your anti-magnetism, passion, and commitment to push.

Now other people prefer to be pulled and/or left alone to follow. They prefer this because they can see you out in front of them, going and being in the places where they are eventually going to get.

A true Leader doesn't just point. A true Leader must be willing to go to the places where they want their people to follow. So go!

But if you just Lead without some tension and a little bit of pull, a little tether attached to your tribe, you'll be the only one out there. They'll stand back and say, "Well, let's see how that works out for him." So, you must pull as you move forward, and then occasionally, when they get afraid and freeze into position, run to the back of the line and give them a push.

Appropriately oscillating between push and pull defines a healthy EQUALibrium (Olver, 2008) and is, in my opinion, the desired state of Balance for an empowering Leader.

But there's another piece to balancing your sense of EQUALibrium.

Instead of mentally constructing your concept of "push" as on the right and "pull" as on the left, while imagining you're the plumb line in the center, let's think of us more as the leveling tool. We're the little bubble in the construction worker's leveler and we're trying to do our dance from within the fluid while bubbling to the top in a state of Balance. Now we're going to imagine our tribe is the fluid, pressing up against and sliding off us, sloshing around and needing our positioning to compare and contrast to so that they might have a sense of self. They are all around us, and we are grounding them by being their air, perSEEved at the top *and* in the middle of their world, making the invisible visible, attainable, and real.

True Balance as a Leader requires both of these understandings, both of these abilities. You must be at the top *and* in the middle.

When you are grounding in the center and letting all of the people swirl around you, they are the chaos. You are the clarity, and your voice becomes the one voice that they can Hear without confusion (Scouller, 2011).

It's important that you not get lost in their confusion. And the only way for that to be true is for you to have a clear mission statement, a clear understanding of what your purpose is as you Lead.

Is your purpose to make money? Is your purpose to make lives better for children around the world? Is your purpose to feed the hungry? Is your purpose to invent the best shoe leather ever invented so that shoes never wear out? Is your purpose to be seen by all your family members as the smartest dude in the family tree?

It really doesn't matter what it is. I am not judging your purpose. I *am* saying, though, if you don't know what your purpose is, you will be a part of the chaotic noise of the crowd and disperse into the middle, a broken bubble that's lost its Balance.

To be at the top, grounded as a leader—the perfectly placed bubble in the leveler's tool—you have to know where the top is. You have to know not just your purpose or your goal. You have to know what it looks like when you get it. You have to hold a vision of what it looks like at the top and a concept of how to be at the top while still holding onto your EQUALibrium.

The dancer "spots the wall" while spinning. I suggest you "spot the people" while Leading them.

State of Balance as a Leader is more than the usual socially understood definition of, "Am I Balanced in my time expenditure in relation to family and work?"

Actually, if you like work more than you like family, I suppose you would be more Balanced by being at work and giving your family small quality moments of time, rather than sitting there with them going, "Gee, okay. I'm giving them fifty percent of my time, and I really hate it."

No. That kind of Balance is better achieved by understanding yourself, understanding what you like to do, what you think is important, and then planning your time accordingly (Management, 2012).

But EQUALity, as I said before, is not sameness. This is a definition error that I had in my own sense of EQUALibrium, and it took me a long time to learn how to individualize the need for push-pull, time allocations, and financial resources so that I could be truly EQUAL by being not the same.

True, if you don't give enough time to your family, they may compare and contrast and decide to leave you. So, be aware. Make your choices with clarity. Know what you want to accomplish, and then accomplish that.

> *"Once we accept our limits, we go beyond them"*
> ~ *Albert Einstein and/ or Brendan Francis*

Make sure to include all the aspects of your life in that picture. Be fully aware and let that awareness include time.

Word of caution: If you choose, "I want to be the richest man in the world so that I can give my family everything they want with ease," by the time you become the richest man in the world, you may not have that family; and the only family that will show up in your face to spend time with you may be the kind of family that goes after the richest men in the world. So the family you've gained to spend your riches on may not be worth more than a dollar or two. EQUALibrium means Balancing from within the whole, not sectioning off one piece at a time so you can accomplish it in bite-sized bits.

Being Balanced is an art of inclusivity (Snyder, 2013).

So, while you worry about push-pull and being in the center of the chaos and being the grounding force, also remember that what you build, so you will become. If you choose to be the richest man in the world in order to give your family great things, you might want to make sure you take them along for the ride because a truly Balanced Leader understands the motivators of the people in his world, and doesn't plan to end up alone, without a following.

Anyone who looks to you for guidance and directions is a follower, even family and potential partners.

They are watching you live, so live well.

If you lose your EQUALibrium, you'll fall on your face, and that's a different role.

Chapter Seven

SENSE SEVEN in the SEVEN SENSES of LEADERSHIP

MYTH #11

This myth—as with most myths—exists in opposite extremes. Myth 1, *"You need a college degree to be successful!"* Myth 2, *"Dropouts and C students run the world!"*

Both myths can be proven or disproven according to a person's wishes. And perhaps that is the definition of a myth: Something debatable.

Solving this debate requires choosing rather than proving. That is because both of these myths can be backed up with lists of success stories that fit the proclamation. For the most part it appears that many historically impressive people like Thomas Edison, Benjamin Franklin, William Shakespeare, Abraham Lincoln, and John D Rockefeller did succeed without proper schooling and were undereducated by today's standards (Burlingame, 1997). However, during these varied time periods, leaving school at a young age was a typical occurrence. Thus, success commonly relied on self-education and a personal commitment to learning.

Pointing to the success of these historical giants as proof of a modern day need for or against education is like holding up an apple to prove oranges are red. The demands of the eras are not comparable.

Financial, educational, historical, and scientific data, along with high-profile opinion makers, can be gathered and faced off to support either position. For example, some of today's unarguably successful highly influential Leaders like Warren Buffet, Howard Stern, Barack Obama, Donald Trump, and Rachel Maddow are all degreed professionals.

With a little bit of work the researcher or espouser can "prove" what they "choose" based on their particular opinion and definition of Leader. These prejudices will lead them to the evidence they will then compile.

Billionaires like Bill Gates, Steve Jobs, and Mark Zuckerberg may be college dropouts; but they discovered their vision, their passion, and peer network while in college (Isaacson, 2015), (Lesinski, 2009), (Lusted, 2011). Surrounding yourself with appropriately skilled and similarly focused people in order to actively realize your vision IS a Leadership trait. Groundbreakers like George Lucas, Ross Perot and Arnold Schwarzenegger (Schwarzenegger, 2012), (Perot, 1996), (Lucas and Kline, 1999), who all managed to complete college degrees also attained highly memorable Leadership success status. And they did that as finishers, not dropouts. So everybody got what they came for—the finishers AND the quitters—they got the inspiration of an educational environment. At this point proponents for either side of Myths 1 or 2 can soapbox with confidence according to their perspective.

The problem isn't so much with the myths as the ambiguity of the terms used with the verbiage of these myths. Words and phrases like "successful" or "run the world" are too vague. Ambiguity encourages the listener to input their own definition and, since it contains their own definition, they generally bypass the inclination to analyze and end up agreeing with the myth.

It is true that in today's world, a small percentage of Leaders hold the wealth. It is also always true. If wealth were commonplace, then it would not be wealth. Its rarity is the point and the reason we try to attain it.

The people who succeed in attaining it are graduates, dropouts, "A" students and "C" students. So why then the "C" students run the world part of the myth?

Exceptions are interesting, especially when they offer hope to the majority. Being a Leader is already an exceptional state so people are looking. And when they look they are often looking for hope. "A" students pepper the high-level well-paid positions globally. In a strange twist of irony, this makes them commonplace, for exceptional people.

Therefore, since "C" students are more common and compose the larger audience, when they seek a Leader to follow, finding one like themselves that has broken through the educational barriers and left a path to follow is newsworthy. This larger audience also makes talking about "C" student Leaders more likely to be written about and published since more people will read your article. And thus it is that the myth propagates.

Researching these education stories of famous innovators is fascinating. Walt Disney left high school, lied about his age, eventually drove an ambulance covered in cartoons, and found Mickey Mouse (Gabler, 2011). The rest is our childhood history. Ray Kroc, who turned McDonald's into the largest food chain, also quit school, lied about his age, and drove an ambulance (Kroc and Anderson, 1992). However, do not be distracted by these details. Both men succeeded despite these bits and pieces of their story. Not because of them.

They had different brains. They had Leader's Brains. They saw and did things in a visionary, hard-working, *emotionally intelligent* way. Like Richard Branson, the famous entrepreneurial dyslexic, their problems with school are a part of their story but not the reason for their success (Fertig, 2013).

Disney, Kroc, and Branson dropped out of school. They saw things differently enough to land at the top of the 20 percent club. But then the same is true of college graduates Oprah Winfrey and Steven Spielberg (who by the way took over 30 years to graduate). School is a part of their story but not the reason for their success. Despite the fact that it could be perSEEved as integral to her success, even Mayim Bialik PhD, one of *The Big Bang Theory's* actresses, likely got the role of a woman with a PhD because of her talent as an actress not the coincidence of her actually having completed graduate school.

That being said, graduate degrees often are required, so pretending otherwise ignores a large section of society. I never would have met and been helped by the famous Dr. Atkins if he hadn't finished school. So some careers that create billionaires, millionaires, life changers that Lead absolutely do require education. Stephen Hawking, Jane Goodall, Carlos Slim, and Joe Jamail all required a high level degree to be the forces they are today (Larsen, 2005), (Greene, 2005), (Martinez, 2013), (F. P. Miller, Vandome, and McBrewster, 2011). These people succeeded in part because of school but it is still—even for them—just a part of the story.

So the question really isn't "Do you need school to be a Leader?" but "Do you want to be a Charles Dickens (quit school) or a Dr. Phil (finished school)?"

If in general you operate well within a system and feel socially connected to your peers at school, in sports or academics, then stay in school and gain the knowledge and networking edge that college will give you. But if you want to marry well, like high school dropout Lady Dianna, or reach star status like Marlon Brando, college may not be your best training ground.

Today, the largest number of super successful drop-out Leaders tend to be celebrities. So make sure you factor that into the 80/20 rule. (Eighty percent of anything is created by 20 percent of the people. This includes money.) The celebrity component to being a high-profile success story is important because uneducated celebrities like Al Pacino, John Travolta, Ryan Gosling, Johnny Depp, Hillary Swank, Seth Rogen, Eminem, Robert Downey Jr., Robert De Niro, Jim Carrey, Roseanne Barr, and the amazing Quentin Tarantino seem to have gotten lucky.

Their lives look glamorous and easy. But this type of career choice requires more study and commitment to self-improvement than a PhD. Celebrities pour money into their own development, their health, their appearance, their skills; they do workshops, classes, and hire coaches etc. And there is no graduation day—just a life of continuing education and commitment. The longer a celebrity is in the business, the more they have to spend to maintain their position. Fame is expensive.

Leaders of any type, "C" students, "A" students, degreed and not, all have to pay attention to the balance between their brain and body. They avail themselves of anything to get the slight edge: exercise, dietary restrictions, and brain-enhancing therapies like neurofeedback, to name a few.

So though some may drop out of school, none drop out of learning and growing. This is true of all of them, your favorite athlete as well. Success is hard work. So bust the myths and follow the truth.

If you are passionate there is a path that suits you, find it, not the myth that opposes your position. It's all made up any way. Be willing to be different if you are different, and don't pretend to be if you are not (Jordan and Whaley, 2007). If you are a member of the 80 percent club, become 20 percent of that 80 percent. No matter where you are, there is a Leader position to fill.

There are no rules to follow, just myths to bust. Because that is what Leaders do, they bust things up a bit and change the rules.

SENSE SEVEN

SCENTS OF SUCCESS

The seventh sense of leadership is the SCENTS of SUCCESS.

You may have expected this SENSE to be called the CENTS of SUCCESS given the image of golden bars and golden coins on the book cover. But that would be too uninspired and myopic.

Consider the minimalist Leader and how his/her picture of SUCCESS would look. It would still be a treasure trove of achievements of course. SUCCESS is always about searching, finding and claiming your treasure aka the goal of intended results. The bars and coins on the cover represent this.

However, in true Leadership the desired treasure is seldom filled with acquisitions and/or money. Those are just wonderful side benefits, glorious to get if you wish to have them, worthy of acquiring, true, lovely to see spilling from your trunk, yes, but NOT the core of the contents in your chest.

A true treasure is filled with achievements: A lifetime of purposeful improvements. And boy, does that ever smell with the constant SCENT of SUCCESS!

Everything has a SCENT. Everything leaves a trail, especially SUCCESS. Unless you exist in a vacuum and are only leading yourself into an implosion of the senses.

Leaders create vacuums; they don't live in them. A vacuum is a source of usable energy for a Leader.

The Universe abhors a vacuum and always seeks to fill the space.

Leaders Lead. They are always on the move. And every time they step forward, they leave an empty space behind in their wake, a vacuum as it were, that somebody else must step into and fill.

If you have a sense for SUCCESS, the SCENT of SUCCESS as a Leader, then what you are aware of at all times is the continued need for motion (Fulton, 1995).

You must always be stepping out of the place you're at, so that someone else can fill in the space behind you. This is different from grounding your energy and calling people to you, different from the sense of Here and now. It's different from FEELing their energy or looking at them or perSEEving their truth.

The SCENTS of SUCCESS are Aromas created by intending and moving and staying alive in your energy as a Leader. All Leaders are in perpetual motion, even as they stand still and call you to them.

Leaders are always emitting and being purposeful, calling and being purposeful, intending and being purposeful (Dudley, 2013). Even family time is done with the SCENT of purpose and intention.

So that seventh sense, that all important culmination of our seven Leadership Sensibilities, is the SCENTS of SUCCESS, that is released by the LEADERSHIP sweat glands. These SCENTS are emitted by purposeful action being applied in every endeavor, by the need to move, grow, and become more.

A Natural Leader naturally knows how to build himself using the world around him and the raw material of his personage. A Learned Leader learns to do the same. In the end, you can't tell one from the other.

Regardless of where you are now you can become anything, through learning. So learn.

A Leader knows he is not stuck at any point in his development, knows that there are many paths to his goal, knows that he doesn't have to be any one thing to become another. And if he doesn't know this, he learns it in order to grow. A Leader is always on the move, always in a state of becoming (Moxley, 2015).

A Leader grows while teaching others how to be in a similar evolutionary state, growing into the place he just vacated.

A Leader with a missing SENSE is never disabled. A Leader uses every circumstance and creates something new, a new SCENT for others to smell. In this case, a Leader would use one SCENSE to take over for the other.

Thus, what was previously considered a limitation becomes a clarifying ingredient and creates progress, a new recipe, a unique formulation for the SCENT of SUCCESS.

This new SCENT of SUCCESS breaks ground and builds an evolutionary path for other differently SCENTED learners to follow.

In other words, whatever you are now—even if you are a follower—you are evolving into something else, either bigger, smaller, happier, sadder, in front, or behind—but always, always, different. So stay on top of your own evolution and do not give anything up to fate or serendipity.

In this way, even if you're not a Leader or are differently SCENTED but want to Lead, all you have to do is use the interested parts of your brain to ride your passion. This will fuel your personality with joy. And joy will ignite you into movement and creativity.

Once your passion infuses you, it brands your SCENT of SUCCESS into your soul and you'll walk with the confidence and direction of a Leader.

And that air of SUCCESS will attract followers, HEIRS to your SUCCESS.

So fuel yourself, so that you can build your own personal SCENTS of SUCCESS and SUCCEED.

But don't be misLed.

Your climb to the top will not be smooth and continuous.

No growth is linear. No one is always strong and focused and headed steadfastly for their goal. Not even Leaders. A Great Leader knows that everybody slumps, so a Great Leader also knows how to refresh, refocus and reset his/her brain, body, soul (Chopra, 2011).

Without this ability to reset Leaders slump. They go from SUCCESS to SUCKSESS.

No Leader is okay with that.

Because slumping SUCKS-ASS!

So Leaders prioritize themselves and Learn what works for them.

Personally, I use Neurofeedback when I need mental strength, heightened focus, and a reigniting of my passion. I also use Neurofeedback to prevent the brain degeneration of aging and maintain my IQ as well as my memory.

Neurofeedback is biofeedback for the brain. It works through observing brain wave activity on a computer screen and then teaching the brain, via sensory feedback, how to improve itself by firing in a more Balanced way (Demos, 2005).

All feedback to the brain is received via our seven senses, even if it arrives from a biofeedback device. And that is what makes me a Leadership Sensibility Brain Expert, Biofeedback for the Brain. I am good at it.

Presently, I am a global thought Leader, sense expert, and feedback loop re-designer for brain challenges around the world.

Unlike the more common approaches to brain change via mood stabilizers, academic studies, social and psychological shame and blame, or support and sell, Neurofeedback is an objective measure that directs improvement without judgment. Neurofeedback, like a Good Leader, gives brains the needed information for SUCCESS and invites them to follow; it never forces (Senior, Lee, and Braeutigam, 2015).

Thus, rather than resist learning—as is the norm for brains and hence people when responding to teacher, parent, authority figure feedback—when using this form of feedback, the *freedom* to follow makes the brain happy to comply.

As mentioned, the information communicated via biofeedback itself is delivered through your senses in the same way that feedback for the brain and body is always received.

Signals are sent through your sensory system using various instruments, like a vibrating toy whose signals run along the FEELing path, a game on your computer screen whose vibrant vibrations and reward sounds travel both the perSEEving and the HEREing now paths. These three senses—SEE, HEAR, FEEL—are the primary colors in the art and science of biofeedback (Rosenbaum, 1989).

Biofeedback-delivered information doesn't directly travel the TASTE TESTING, ODORE of ADORE or EQUALibrium roads, but it does do construction work upon them.

Feedback functions within the brain like a spider web composed of neurons sharing gossip. Everything is connected and affected. Neurofeedback informs the brain at lightning speed with unparalleled efficiency, rather like tickling a spider's web at the farthest corner from where the spider sits waiting many feet away. Then, despite the subtleness of the touch and the obvious attenuation of the vibration due to the distance the wave must traverse along those silken threads, the spider is still alerted and driven to move.

Everything is connected through this type of neuronal web. A neuronal web that interacts with and weaves together, instincts with desires, fueled and funneled by neurons and intentions. Intentionally building our SCENTS of SUCCESS begins when we stop arguing about nature versus nurture and embrace them both at the same time.

Because what you think, so shall you fire, the related neurons in order to become, create, and have.

To be effective biofeedback can send signals via any of the senses. To be purposeful, precise, and SUCCESSFUL is a little trickier.

The system I use relies on perSEEving and HEREing, but the way I use it leans heavily on HEREing alone. With this one sensory feedback path, I am able to inform all the senses and invite each of them to help me improve brain function, neuron to neuron, glial cell to glial cell, hope to results.

This use of one sense to change the others models and matches hijacking vision to improve Balance. I, however, don't hijack vision to improve Balance but initiate sounds to improve senses, all of them, even the SCENTS of SUCCESS.

Once attended to, the instructions received by the brain from those Neurofeedback-driven reward tones—reward tones with no moral imperative or implied judgment—are followed.

The brain, which has an instinctual drive to restore and improve its own state of EQUALibrium, EQUALizes.

As I explained, I use Neurofeedback to heal brains around the globe.

So obviously I would be foolish to not also help myself when needed. Fortunately, I am not foolish, anymore.

And because I am no longer foolish (that is another book) and have Learned how to Lead, I also use Neurofeedback to help my own EQUALibrium EQUALize.

This Leadership Sensibility brain-changing expertise was a fortunate skill to have a few years back.

One night I was awakened from my sleep by a loud popping sound coming from somewhere in my right hemisphere. I was immediately overwhelmed by a spinning world and body-wide nausea. I thought I was about to die. But since I wasn't dead yet, I wanted to at least get the world to stop rolling and spinning before I met the reaper.

I belly crawled down the stairs toward my Neurofeedback equipment, and with a good deal of fumbling, between bouts of vomiting, I managed to set myself up. I had no idea what type of instruction my brain needed, no idea what would work, and I wasn't in any brain state to analyze the situation so I just did what usually helped me. I put a sensor on my sensory motor strip and another on my frontal lobes.

Since, as I said, I didn't know what else to do and was choosing what usually made me feel happy, I cranked the reward goal up really high. Happy feels akin to fast processing and higher frequencies process faster. So I had the computer give my brain the feedback, "GO FASTER!"

I figured I couldn't feel happy without a stationary world beneath my feet so, maybe, my brain getting happy would make my perSEption of the world behave. It was as good a theory as any.

At this juncture I had not worked with vertigo or stroke; and since I suspected I was dealing with both, I was pretty much making it up out of habits and hopes while attending to my own experiential sensations. I believed my senses would warn me if I was making it worse.

I didn't make it worse. I made it better.

Neurofeedback helped and I was able to sleep a bit. I did a little more in the morning and the results were beneficial enough to survive work all that day.

However, in the weeks that followed, the vertigo kept returning so I tried to stop it by spotting the wall and running to my Neurofeedback to instruct my brain happy.

At one point I even considered making a plumb line for my glasses, but I was afraid the swinging of the string would make me vomit. I couldn't manage a leveler as I didn't have the needed materials so I felt a little without choices. Then I remembered one of the stories in the book *The Brain that Changes Itself* by Norman Doidge (Doidge, 2008). It was about a group of scientists that helped a woman with a form of body blindness that made her warble and fall. To help her stand erect, the scientists used a tongue device that basically made it so that her tongue could see. The device identified the environment via different frequencies based on the different items in the room. It worked. Initially the effect was very short lived, but with each successive use of the device the effect time grew longer. Her brain simply learned new ways to control her body so that she could navigate the world.

Unfortunately, I did not have one of these fancy devices. Since my brain was now in a good enough state to analyze I considered the concept and asked myself, "What can I use to mirror their results? Where can I find enough nerve endings and touch receptors to equal the tongue?" And then it came to me, "The skin!"

I designed a cost-free method. Whenever the room began to spin, I simply widened my focus over the back of my body—took a moment to FEEL my epidermis—and positioned my skin against a wall. I literally shut down my other senses and saw with my skin. It worked! The moment I would FEEL my contact with the wall, the stationary world relaxed into place.

This FEEL method was much better than using my vision had been because it was softer, more expansive, and less laser like.

Using my vision had required angry precision and felt a lot like I imagine it feels to throw a spear into a charging shark. You stop the problem but are now tethered to it and have to pull it from the water or drag it along behind you while simultaneously trying not to get eaten by the rest of its friends.

The anger, exertion, and attention to detail is exhausting.

To help you understand the difference, let me explain how I experienced using vision to stop vertigo. Whenever the room began to spin, I would sit up and throw anger at an imaginary bull's-eye on my wall or door. I would do this with immediate laser-like intensity in order to anchor the world to the chosen location in front of me. Conversely, my new approach of shifting focus to the skin on my back in touch with the wall felt diffuse and gentle, self-loving instead of angry and hateful.

Using FEELing was like cocooning myself in place and coercing the world into stillness.

Since this approach brought the senses away from perSEEving with anger—an act which always creates negative feedback loops that actually reinforce conditions and aberrant states rather than heal them—the vertigo just went away, for longer and longer periods of time.

It wasn't just tethered or anchored in place by my eyes while I carefully walked around keeping my head still. It was gone. What a relief—for everyone in my house!

My family and friends had found the anger frightening and shrunk away. We were all happy to have me no longer be scary.

How is such a simple solution possible? How does it work?

It's simple.

The FEEL of my skin against the wall sent messages which changed the paths my brain used to identify Balance, changed the way my brain focused, felt, and believed. I taught my brain, through external feedback, how to use FEELing to more expansively perSEEv, and in the process discovered a healing, for us all. I ended up more connected to my environment, my family, and friends.

I wanted it gone for good, not just for longer and longer periods of time. So I researched the location of those semicircular canals and created a Neurofeedback protocol that included placing the sensor in a brain location adjacent to the cochlea. I believed using Neurofeedback to reeducate the brain (Collura, 2014)and its Balance system might completely cement the stationary world into position and stop the rollercoaster of healing. It did.

I got better, Led myself back to health, and then Led others.

This combo has worked for me and everyone I have thus far Led.

In fact, this type of nature-embraces-nurture combo is how I do things around the world. I teach people to work with their environment and use Neurofeedback to solidify the results.

This vertigo correction discovery happened because I conferred with an expert via an expert's story in a book written by someone with rubber to the road. I appreciate writers, especially science writers.

When these professionals take the time to tell a case story, we have the opportunity to steer our own mental and physical health. I learned a new trick, though I had to individualize and reshape it. I evolved a new brain, just as you are doing now. I replaced my tongue and their special tongue gizmo, first with my eyes and then with my skin and Neurofeedback,

I discovered and invented, all because something in me broke just enough for me to have to learn how to make it better. Because I ended up with vertigo I gained subjective knowledge and became my own expert, learned to Lead my brain to EQUALize itself, and deliver me to a new, better state of EQUALibrium.

All this happened because forward motion is the only direction I take. This is what it is to be a Leader.

In part, it is because I Led myself that I am better at Leading you. And the practice of Leading has sharpened my Leadership Sensibilities.

This type of hands-on Learning and self-correction, augmented by experts and education, has made me very unique in my field.

I am especially gifted with Neurofeedback, cognitive restructuring, and creative Play.

Now that I have Learned all this, I know that I could easily have helped Oliver Sacks' patient without a plumb line or extended horizontal levels attached to his glasses. If I met him in my present, that is.

But without his past and the concept of the glasses plumb line, the horizontal levelers, Norman Doidge's woman and the tongue sensor for Balance, I wouldn't know now what I couldn't have known then.

I guess that is why we learn and grow like our ever-changing brains, to evolve into sharers of information.

So Oliver Sacks and his patient never met me. I never knew that elderly man, that brilliant self-healer, until he became a story in Oliver Sacks' book. So I couldn't help him and he had to Lead himself, and also Oliver Sacks.

Just as I had to Lead myself, my patients, my children, and you, who Lead others. The circle of life spins while the players change places, eternally.

IIIIIIIIIIIIIIIIIIIIIIIIIIIIIIIIIIIIIIIIIIIII ▼ ▼ ▼ IIIIIIIIIIIIIIIIIIIIIIIIIIIIIIIIIIIIIIIIIIIIIIIIII

LEADER: Billionaire JEFF BEZOS (1964–), founder and CEO of Amazon.com, is responsible for most of the 42 million dollars raised towards building *The Clock of Long Now* which is designed to run for 10,000 years and to be buried deep in the Sierra Diablo Mountains on Bezos' land (Lac, 2012).

Bezos is an engineer and computer scientist with a mechanical genius and an eccentric taste for life. For example, Bezos has spent years attempting to privatize space travel and engages in unusual pastimes like recovering the engines from the famed Apollo 11, which he found on the bottom of the Atlantic Ocean (Hitt, Ireland, and Hoskisson, 2014).

Bezos, like all multi-billionaires, gets his share of criticism. But one thing is evident by his inventions and unusual passions: Bezos, who wants to put hotels and amusement parks in space with colonies of 2 to 3 million people, Leads people.

IIIIIIIIIIIIIIIIIIIIIIIIIIIIIIIIIIIIIIIIIIII ▲ ▲ ▲ IIIIIIIIIIIIIIIIIIIIIIIIIIIIIIIIIIIIIIIIIIIIIIIII

All Leaders are eccentric because they do what they think is right!

If Jeff Bezos succeeds in changing the definition of what is "possible" the people he Leads will get to "Go where no man (but William Shatner) has gone before!" And in the process he will make more history, and an awful lot of money.

All Leaders are eccentric because they perSEEv possibilities where others do not!

The SCENTS of SUCCESS is comprised of three things

One: A clear understanding of movement in the vacuum.

Two: A clearly defined idea of what SUCCESS smells like so that you can step into it.

Three: A firm conviction that when you have what you designed as a successful life, you will immerse in the SCENTS of completion and accomplishment; you will not let anybody else's definition prevent you from breathing in and being delighted by your own SCENTS of SUCCESS.

Leaders ask the questions that will get them to the desired answer. For example a Leader would ask, "Where is the money?" and not "Why don't I have any?" A Leader would ask, "How can I feel strong?" and not "Why do I feel weak?" or "How do I stop the spinning and make the world stay in place?" not "Why won't it stop spinning?

Leaders are headed into answers that create movement forward. They ask the questions that Lead them there, to the next, best thing.

At one point I asked myself, "How do I get exercise and spontaneous joy at the same time?" I found many answers: "Dancing, singing, joke telling, and play." And I did them all.

I used dancing for flexibility and cardio health and singing to oxygenate my cells and lift my spirit. I told jokes and practiced standup comedy to exercise my communication skills and audience perSEEVing. I used play to heal children with joy and exuberance, which heals me. Play keeps me young and prevents degeneration. It also keeps me ready to squeal with delight at any given moment. Imagine spending your life at the ready for fun!

My soul is lifted by all of these. That is how I know I asked and answered some very good questions. For me, having the freedom to exercise these choices is my definition of SUCCESS.

Knowing how to reset and refresh while connecting to life's universal answers is a LEADERship must! Many Leaders use mediation, hypnosis, competitive sports, supplements, and more. There are many paths, and none of them work all the time, every time. Some paths get worn out and need to be replaced. The important thing is to find your most powerful current option and use that. Build a library of choices and tell people about them.

Counter to what the movie *The Secret* led you to believe, Leaders share their knowledge (Heriot, 2007). In fact, sharing their expertise is one of their greatest pleasures. They love this. There are many descriptive terms for people in positions of power that keep and use secrets. In my opinion, Leader is not one of them, because Leaders Lead.

But they want you to HEAR them. Be HERE and HEAR or they stop sharing. Because Leaders are busy, moving forward, they don't like to waste time sharing with no one.

Unfortunately, followers can't always HEAR it HERE and now, because they are distracted with desperation. Desperate people seek to be saved, not told they have work to do. Desperation is exhausting and as such makes them resistant to the very change they are seeking. Thus they HEAR a morphed version of what is actually being said. In this state of resistance and desperation, a follower will Hear falsehoods and therefore think "the truth" is not being shared. However, the answers are age old and have always been known, shared, and offered up freely by Leader after Leader.

Since this referred-to state of desperation makes answers hard to HEAR and information is generally misunderstood as it gets misconstrued and passed on, misshapen followers often find themselves in a cognitive conundrum. Thus repetition of information via every one of the Seven Senses is required for a Leader to Lead. As Leaders seek to help, again and again, the information is misconstrued and passed on misshapen. Leaders will stay the course and accept the responsibility of repackaging their message. But even repackaged, the core information must remain consistent because Leaders have something to say. Make note, Leaders take the blame for the mistakes in the gossip chain. It is the Leaders who have their reputational neck in the noose.

Great Leaders share their message with repetition, with variety, with a willingness to knock on the door of opportunity. Leaders Lead till others follow, by explaining and re-explaining, over and over again. A Leader's job is to always and forever be clearing up confusion, breaking down resistance, and getting their message across, to help you grow.

A Leader is like a parent, doomed for extinction. They help you grow to let you go.

This is why they say it is lonely to be a Leader.

This is also why Great Leaders confer with other Leaders for community and inspiration. They seek each other's advice. They get help in decoding and understanding the vibrations of their people. They problem solve together the dilemma of resistant followers who stay in the fold yet fight the information. Even Leaders seek to be Led, to grow greater, achieve more, and Lead you higher.

Leaders share their *secret* recipes of SUCCESS because secrets are counterproductive to growth in the evolution and discovery of new formulations, new achievements, and new SCENTS for SUCCESS.

Oh, and one more thing. There is no "Follow Before" date. Leaders Lead forever.

Success happens in the present, past, and future. To be a SUCCESSful Leader you must stay aware and always be Leading, Leaders. They copy you.

The belief about you and the things that will be copied, as well as what will be perSEEved as true in regards to your past, present, and future (or death) depend greatly on how you exit the limelight.

Robin Williams (1951-2014) is a good example of a person everyone saw as highly successful, and yet his ending changes the story (Dougan, 1999).

Despite his bouts of rehab, marriages, and heart problems, Robin Williams seemed happy, spontaneous, and alive with hilarity to the people watching him perform. But his last act was one of suicide. It conjures up images of a man with the desperate need to die, so desperate that he would use a belt to strangle himself. This ending lays a blanket of darkness over his entire life. A Leader's suicide can leave the followers FEELing confused and betrayed. Despite the fact that Robin Williams was a senior with several diseases and a dying body, his ending leaves a void, a void that others might want to follow.

My job includes suicide prevention. I have prevented two suicides inspired by Robin. When you are a Leader, people follow.

If your goal is to make people laugh, it is best not to end the story by making them want to die. So understand that if you choose to be a Leader, it is a lifelong commitment to your people.

How you quit determines your legacy and your effectiveness. So if your SCENT of SUCCESS leaves people with a SCENT of SUCKSESS you have defeated your purpose. Lead only where you want them to follow, because they will follow.

Remember, nature abhors a vacuum. So look to the horizon, choose the trajectory, and step forward. This will create a vacuum behind you.

> *"The reasonable man adapts himself to the world; the unreasonable one persists in trying to adapt the world to himself. Therefore all progress depends on the unreasonable man."*
>
> *~ George Bernard Shaw*

Others will follow.

The SCENTS of SUCCESS encompasses the concept that leaders move the mountain.

That old saying, "If the mountain won't come to Muhammad, then Muhammad must go to the mountain," published back in the 1600's in a book of English proverbs, shows how long we have known the SECRETS that never really were secret. This saying has value and indicates a Leader's willingness to do what it takes to make a connection. However, I think for our purposes it is better to do a little reshaping and rewrite that age-old truth using someone other than Muhammad.

Let us build upon the concept and say, "Someone with Leadership Sensibilities, someone like Steve Jobs, will go to the mountain to dislodge it from its stuckness, but then pass it in his wake if the mountain refuses to be moved. Someone like Steve is not stopped by the impenetrableness of the mountain; and if the mountain wants to go where Steve is, the mountain better follow."

However, don't misunderstand this to mean that a Leader gets there "by any means."

Leaders have a vision (Metz, 2011), and that vision includes the path they are willing to walk upon. This lack of confusion or distraction from their mission is where their strength to never fully burn out comes from.

A Leader doesn't get there "by any means" because a leader has ironclad ethics, though their ethics may be unique and out of step from the norm, that is the point, and they are untaintable.

So a Leader doesn't "get there by any means," but a Leader does "get there." They never quit. They don't drop the goal and head down a dissimilar path. They just reroute with the same goal in mind. Like your GPS guiding you on a new adventure, a Leader notices the error in judgment and makes a new map.

A Leader doesn't over worry about what the market wants. A Leader knows that the market has been misLed.

If there is no road, they pave one. No industry, they make one. No tool, they invent one. Whatever they need, they create the solution.

A Leader is propelled by their passion. People are attracted to that and follow. However, this attraction must be built and will require varying amounts of time to fully blaze. If the world feels no need for the Leader's chosen passion, the Leader may experience a period of aloneness, Leading only themselves.

But a Leader Leads. So they sing from their soap box until their passion fuels a desire in the world around them. Even when there is no need, they create one.

Leaders find this easy and unavoidable because their passion fuels them, and they need to Lead on the subject of their passion.

So they Lead according to their own needs and then shape the world around them. Progress.

Sometimes it appears as if the Leader shaped themselves to match the market's needs, so sometimes the truth is not evident because coincidentally what the market wanted to buy was the same as what the Leader wanted to sell. They call this timing. I call it *people heard your song and turned in your direction.*

It is more than timing. It is the unseen parts of the path walked and made visible.

In fact, Leaders never bend to the need of the population. They *do* listen and fill their people's desires in order to share their message, but they don't bend or falsely promise just to hook a person into their fold. That is a salesman, not a Leader.

Leaders Lead from integrity and vision, and the population follows the Lead of the Leader. These are the qualities you must cultivate if you wish to Lead the world somewhere new and better.

So understand, it is the followers who redesign their need, not the Leader. And this is as it should be since the follower is following in order to Learn what the Leader knows. Learning is another word for reshaping oneself.

Standing firm to your vision while learning how to move and teach and reshape others and then doing THAT!

That's a Leader.

Because Leaders are always moving. They understand that brains are problem-solving machines. So they fuel their machine by solving problems (Williams-Boyd, 2002). They understand that, like the alternator must be running to power a car battery, the brain must be solving problems to fire a connection and grow a network.

Networks increase strength so Leaders build networks within and without. Thus, to be a Leader you must be building—your network and yourself.

Take a daily CENSUS of your people, your reasons, and responsibilities. Then grow. Heighten your vision, your energy, and your bar!

Always be learning, sharing, serving, and caring.

Raise mankind up higher by filling yourself with the LEADERSHIP SENSIBILITIES of intention and purposeful action.

Be constant and consistent. Be flexible and warm. Be it all.

THAT IS LEADERSHIP!

Moving mountains of people to a higher summit.

Because the SCENTS OF SUCCESS smell like love.

A SIMPLE SEVEN-STEP SUMMARY FOR THE SEVEN SENSES OF LEADERSHIP

STEP ONE

Ask a question.

STEP TWO

SEE. SMELL, TASTE and TOUCH as you observe and analyze the ingredients.

STEP THREE

Insist on a state of EQUALibrium by BALANCing your inner and outer worlds while defining the goal with a SENSE of SUCCESS. Use this definition to formulate an answer.

STEP FOUR

Share what you think with others while simultaneously experiencing their resonance for (or against) your words via all SEVEN of these SENSES.

STEP FIVE

Revamp and rewrite your answers while holding true to your own definition of SUCCESS. The act of speaking out to others changes the ingredients and hence the story. The question evolves. Thus your answers must also evolve. Now share these.

STEP SIX

Infuse your listeners to take an action by creating an action to take. This must be one you passionately agree with. Act together, as one body/brain, sensory system universe. Lead from within.

STEP SEVEN

Now regroup and step out of the chaos for a moment. Ask a new question. Repeat ad infinitum.

IN SUMMARY

Leaders are neither born nor made they are just the ones

taking the Lead, moment to moment, time and again.

So if you want to be better at Leading, Lead.

And take your Leadership Sensibilities with you.

REFERENCES

1. Achterberg, J. (1994). *Rituals of Healing: Using Imagery for Health and Wellness*. Bantam Books.

2. Allen, D. (2011). *Mahatma Gandhi*. Reaktion Books.

3. Amen, D. G. (2009). *Change Your Brain, Change Your Life: Revised and Expanded Edition: The breakthrough programme for conquering anxiety, depression, anger and obsessiveness*. Hachette UK.

4. April, K. A., Macdonald, R., and Vriesendorp, S. (2000). *Rethinking Leadership*. Juta and Company Ltd.

5. Arbib, M. A. (2003). *The Handbook of Brain Theory and Neural Networks*. MIT Press.

6. Arden, J. B. (2010). *Rewire Your Brain: Think Your Way to a Better Life*. John Wiley and Sons.

7. Arden, J. B. (2012). *AARP Rewire Your Brain: Think Your Way to a Better Life*. John Wiley and Sons.

8. *Arts Management*. (1999). Radius Group, Incorporated.

9. Arwood, E. L., and Kaulitz, C. (2007). *Learning with a Visual Brain in an Auditory World: Visual Language Strategies for Individuals with Autism Spectrum Disorders*. AAPC Publishing.

10. Ascher, M. S., and Levounis, P. (2015). *The Behavioral Addictions*. American Psychiatric Pub.

11. Baars, B. J., and Gage, N. M. (2010). *Cognition, Brain, and Consciousness: Introduction to Cognitive Neuroscience*. Academic Press.

12. Baethmann, A., Go, K. G., and Unterberg, A. (2013). *Mechanisms of Secondary Brain Damage*. Springer Science and Business Media.

13. Baumeister, R. F., and Bushman, B. J. (2013). *Social Psychology and Human Nature, Comprehensive Edition*. Cengage Learning.

14. Bear, M. F., Connors, B. W., and Paradiso, M. A. (2007). *Neuroscience*. Lippincott Williams and Wilkins.

15. Begley, S., and Davidson, R. (2012). *The Emotional Life of Your Brain: How Its Unique Patterns Affect the Way You Think, Feel, and Live - and How You Can Change Them*. Hachette UK.

16. Bernstein. (2000). *Modern Physics*. Pearson Education.

17. Bernstein, D. (2010). *Essentials of Psychology*. Cengage Learning.

18. BlindfoldActivation. (2014). *Midbrain Activation: An Amazing Method to Let Your Child Have SUPER-INTUITION*. Out of the Box Indie Publisher.

19. Bogue, E. G. (1985). *The enemies of leadership: lessons for leaders in education*. Phi Delta Kappa Educational Foundation.

20. Bono, E. de. (2015). *The Mechanism of Mind: Understand how your mind works to maximise memory and creative potential*. Random House.

21. Bourne, S. K., Eckhardt, C. A., Sheth, S. A., and Eskandar, E. N. (2012). Mechanisms of deep brain stimulation for obsessive compulsive disorder: effects upon cells and circuits. *Frontiers in Integrative Neuroscience, 6*. http://doi.org/10.3389/fnint.2012.00029

22. Brand, S. (2004). *Good People, Bad People*. Schreiber Pub.

23. Braverman, E. R. (2013). *Younger Brain, Sharper Mind: A 6-Step Plan for Preserving and Improving Memory and Attention at Any Age from America's Brain Doctor*. Rodale.

24. Brian, S. J. (2010). *Forensics: Chemistry and Crime*. Benchmark Education Company.

25. Brillat-Savarin. (1925). *The Physiology of Taste*. Courier Corporation.

26. Brodal, P. (2016). *The Central Nervous System*. Oxford University Press.

27. Brown, T. (2012). *Physiological Psychology*. Elsevier.

28. Bryant, B. J., and Knights, K. M. (2011). *Pharmacology for Health Professionals*. Elsevier Australia.

29. Buijs, R. M., and Swaab, D. F. (2013). *Autonomic Nervous System: Handbook of Clinical Neurology (Series editors: Aminoff, Boller, Swaab)*. Newnes.

30. Burby, L. N. (1999). *Electrical Storms*. The Rosen Publishing Group.

31. Burlingame, M. (1997). *The Inner World of Abraham Lincoln*. University of Illinois Press.

32. Byers, A. (2005). *Oskar Schindler: Saving Jews from the Holocaust*. Enslow.

33. Calvert, M., and MD, D. R. D. (2010). *Navigating Smell and Taste Disorders*. Demos Medical Publishing.

34. Carson, R. E. (2012). *The Brain Fix: What's the Matter with Your Gray Matter: Improve Your Memory, Moods, and Mind*. Health Communications, Inc.

35. Carter, A. (1995). *Mahatma Gandhi: A Selected Bibliography*. Greenwood Publishing Group.

36. Carter, D. K. E., and Seifert, D. C. M. (2012). *Learn Psychology*. Jones and Bartlett Publishers.

37. Carter, L., Ulrich, D., and Goldsmith, M. (2012). *Best Practices in Leadership Development and Organization Change: How the Best Companies Ensure Meaningful Change and Sustainable Leadership*. John Wiley and Sons.

38. Carter, R., Aldridge, S., Page, M., and Parker, S. (2014). *The Human Brain Book*. DK Publishing (Dorling Kindersley).

39. Champney, T. H. (2015). *Essential Clinical Neuroanatomy*. John Wiley and Sons.

40. Chapman, C. (2001). *Eureka!: Success in Science. 2R.* Heinemann.

41. Chapman, S. B., and Kirkland, S. (2014). *Make Your Brain Smarter: Increase Your Brain's Creativity, Energy, and Focus.* Simon and Schuster.

42. Chopra, D. (2011). *The Soul of Leadership: Unlocking Your Potential for Greatness.* Random House.

43. Clark, R. K. (2005). *Anatomy and Physiology: Understanding the Human Body.* Jones and Bartlett Learning.

44. Cohn, J., and Moran, J. (2011). *Why Are We Bad at Picking Good Leaders A Better Way to Evaluate Leadership Potential.* John Wiley and Sons.

45. Colbert, D. (2003). *Deadly Emotions: Understand the Mind-Body-Spirit Connection That Can Heal or Destroy You.* Thomas Nelson Inc.

46. Coles, R. (2010). *The Story of Ruby Bridges.* Scholastic Inc.

47. Collura, T. F. (2014). *Technical Foundations of Neurofeedback.* Routledge.

48. Congress, U. S. (2010). *Congressional Record, V. 151, PT. 17, October 7 to 26, 2005.* Government Printing Office.

49. Conn, P. M. (2008). *Neuroscience in Medicine.* Springer Science and Business Media.

50. Constantini, N., and Hackney, A. C. (2013). *Endocrinology of Physical Activity and Sport: Second Edition.* Springer Science and Business Media.

51. Coon, D., and Mitterer, J. O. (2008). *Introduction to Psychology: Gateways to Mind and Behavior.* Cengage Learning.

52. Cooper, S. (2012). *Brilliant Leader 2e: What the best leaders know, do and say.* Pearson UK.

53. Corradi, M. (2013). *Heal Yourself: Practical Methods On How to Heal Yourself From Any Disease Using the Power of the Subconscious Mind and Natural Medicine.* John Hunt Publishing.

54. Covey, S. R. (1999). *The 7 Habits of Highly Effective People*. New York.

55. Cowen, V. S. (2015). *Pathophysiology for Massage Therapists A Functional Approach*. F.A. Davis.

56. Cytowic, R. E. (2012). *Synesthesia: A Union of the Senses*. Springer Science and Business Media.

57. Damasio, A. R. (1999). *The Feeling of what Happens: Body and Emotion in the Making of Consciousness*. Harcourt Incorporated.

58. Dass, R. (2010). *Be Here Now*. Harper Collins.

59. Davaa, B., and Falorni, L. (2004). *The Story of the Weeping Camel*.

60. Davidson, J. (2001). *Stress Management*. Breathing Space Institute.

61. Davis, K. L., and Neuropsychopharmacology, A. C. of. (2002). *Neuropsychopharmacology: The Fifth Generation of Progress : an Official Publication of the American College of Neuropsychophar-macology*. Lippincott Williams and Wilkins.

62. Demos, J. N. (2005). *Getting Started with Neurofeedback*. W. W. Norton and Company.

63. Dere, E. (2012). *Gap Junctions in the Brain: Physiological and Pathological Roles*. Academic Press.

64. Dispenza, J. (2008). *Evolve Your Brain: The Science of Changing Your Mind*. Health Communications, Inc.

65. Doidge, N. (2008). *The Brain That Changes Itself: Stories of Personal Triumph from the Frontiers of Brain Science*. Penguin UK.

66. Domany, E. (1996). *Models of Neural Networks III: III*. Springer Science and Business Media.

67. Donaldson, M. (2009). *Ruby Bridges*. Lerner Publications.

68. Dougan, A. (1999). *Robin Williams: A Biography*. Perseus Books Group.

69. Doyle-Portillo, and PASTORINO. (2005). *Aie - What Is Psychology*. Wadsworth.

70. Dudley, J. (2013). *LeadeReliability: Where Leadership, Culture, and Profitability Collide*. iUniverse.

71. Dunnett, S. B., Bentivoglio, M., Björklund, A., and Hökfelt, T. (2004). *Dopamine*. Elsevier.

72. Duvoisin, R. C., and Sage, J. (2001). *Parkinson's Disease: A Guide for Patient and Family*. Lippincott Williams and Wilkins.

73. Elsner, R., and Farrands, B. (2012). *Leadership Transitions: How Business Leaders Take Charge in New Roles*. Kogan Page Publishers.

74. Enderle, J. D., Bronzino, J. D., and Blanchard, S. M. (2005). *Introduction to Biomedical Engineering*. Academic Press.

75. Evans, J. R. (2007). *Handbook of Neurofeedback: Dynamics and Clinical Applications*. CRC Press.

76. Fahey, T. D., Insel, P. M., and Roth, W. T. (2007). *Fit and Well: Core Concepts and Labs for Physical Fitness*. McGraw-Hill.

77. Fertig, D. (2013). *Richard Branson*. Raintree.

78. Finzel, H. (2012). *The Top Ten Leadership Commandments*. David C Cook.

79. Forest, S. A., and Light, A. (1999). *The Tranquility System: Instant Relief from Stress*. Trafford Publishing.

80. Freberg, L. (2009). *Discovering Biological Psychology*. Cengage Learning.

81. Freeman, C. (2007). *Never Panic*. Author House.

82. Friedman, H. L., and Hartelius, G. (2015). *The Wiley-Blackwell Handbook of Transpersonal Psychology*. John Wiley and Sons.

83. Friis, E. P. and C. D. of H. S.-C. S. U. L. B. R. H., Seaward, B. L., and Dayer-Berenson, D. U.-C. of N. and H. P. L. (2013). *Managing Stress*. Jones and Bartlett Publishers.

84. Fulkerson, M. (2013). *The First Sense: A Philosophical Study of Human Touch*. MIT Press.

85. Fulton, R. (1995). *Common Sense Leadership: A Handbook for Success as a Leader*. Ten Speed Press.

86. Gabler, N. (2011). *Walt Disney: The Biography*. Aurum Press, Limited.

87. Gallace, A., and Spence, C. (2014). *In Touch with the Future: The Sense of Touch from Cognitive Neuroscience to Virtual Reality*. OUP Oxford.

88. Gardner, C. (2006). *The Pursuit of Happyness* (Film tie-in edition edition). New York: Amistad.

89. Gates, P. (2010). *Clinical Neurology: A Primer*. Elsevier Australia.

90. Gazzaniga, M. S. (2004). *The Cognitive Neurosciences*. MIT Press.

91. Giraldo, J., and Pin, J.-P. (2011). *G Protein-Coupled Receptors: From Structure to Function*. Royal Society of Chemistry.

92. Goldstein, D. S. (2008). *Adrenaline and the Inner World: An Introduction to Scientific Integrative Medicine*. JHU Press.

93. Goleman, D., Boyatzis, R., and McKee, A. (2013). *Primal Leadership: Unleashing the Power of Emotional Intelligence*. Harvard Business Press.

94. Grandin, T., and Panek, R. (2013). *The Autistic Brain: Thinking Across the Spectrum*. Houghton Mifflin Harcourt.

95. Gray, J. A. (1987). *The Psychology of Fear and Stress*. CUP Archive.

96. Greaves, S. (2003). *Twelfth Night*. Shakespeare Comic Books.

97. Greene, M. (2005). *Jane Goodall: A Biography*. Greenwood Publishing Group.

98. Greenfield, N. S., and Sternbach, R. A. (1972). *Handbook of psychophysiology*. Holt, Rinehart and Winston.

99. Greenstein, B., and Greenstein, A. (2007). *Concise Clinical Pharmacology*. Pharmaceutical Press.

100. Haggai, J. E. (2009). *The Influential Leader: 12 Steps to Igniting Visionary Decision Making*. Harvest House Publishers.

101. Haines, D. E. (2010). *Lippincott's Illustrated QandA Review of Neuroscience.* Lippincott Williams and Wilkins.

102. Haken, H. (2007). *Brain Dynamics: An Introduction to Models and Simulations.* Springer Science and Business Media.

103. Hallam, R. S. (1989). *Tinnitus: Living with the Ringing in Your Ears.* Thorsons.

104. Hall, M., and Halliday, T. (1998). *Behaviour and Evolution.* Springer Science and Business Media.

105. Hart, C. (2008). *Secrets of Serotonin, Revised Edition: The Natural Hormone That Curbs Food and Alcohol Cravings, Reduces Pain, and Elevates Your Mood.* Macmillan.

106. Henry, J. L., and Wilson, P. H. (2002). *Tinnitus: A Self-management Guide for the Ringing in Your Ears.* Allyn and Bacon.

107. Herbert, E. (2014). *Robin Williams - When the Laughter Stops 1951-2014.* John Blake Publishing.

108. Heriot, D. (2007). *The Secret.*

109. Heyning, P. van de, and Punte, A. K. (2010). *Cochlear Implants and Hearing Preservation.* Karger Medical and Scientific Publishers.

110. Hicks, E. (2014). *Lasik Surgery: The Good, The Bad And The Ugly About Lasik Eye Surgery, Lasic Side Effects, Lasik Procedure And Much More.* Booktango.

111. Hitt, M. A., Ireland, R. D., and Hoskisson, R. E. (2014). *Strategic Management: Concepts: Competitiveness and Globalization.* Cengage Learning.

112. Hoffman, B. B. (2013). *Adrenaline.* Harvard University Press.

113. Hook, J. R. (2009). *The Leadership Touch: The Search for a Rare Quality.* iUniverse.

114. Hunter, M. R. (2012). *Reflections of Body Image in Art Therapy: Exploring Self Through Metaphor and Multi-media.* Jessica Kingsley Publishers.

115. Isaacson, W. (2015). *Steve Jobs: The Exclusive Biography*. Abacus.

116. Jacobs, E. E., Schimmel, C. J., Masson, R. L. L., and Harvill, R. L. (2015). *Group Counseling: Strategies and Skills*. Cengage Learning.

117. James, W. (2007). *The Principles of Psychology*. Cosimo, Inc.

118. Jarvis, P., and Watts, M. (2012). *The Routledge International Handbook of Learning*. Routledge.

119. Jay, J. K. (2009). *The Inner Edge: The 10 Practices of Personal Leadership*. ABC-CLIO.

120. Jeremy, N. (2006). *The Ten Management PEPs: Plain English Principles for Being a Great People Manager*. AuthorHouse.

121. Jordan, A., and Whaley, L. (2007). *Investigating Your Career*. Cengage Learning.

122. Joseph, R. (2001). *Sexuality: Female Evolution anderotica*. University Press.

123. Jr, R. P. H. (1995). *The Neurobiology of Cocaine: Cellular and Molecular Mechanisms*. CRC Press.

124. Junarso, T. (2009). *Leadership Greatness: Best Practices to Become a Great Leader*. iUniverse.

125. Karczmar, A. G., and Eccles, J. C. (2012). *Brain and Human Behavior*. Springer Science and Business Media.

126. Kaufman, D. M. (2007). *Clinical Neurology for Psychiatrists*. Elsevier Health Sciences.

127. Keller, H. (1985). *Teacher: Anne Sullivan Macy : a Tribute by the Foster-child of Her Mind*. Greenwood Press.

128. Kemmerer, D. (2014). *Cognitive Neuroscience of Language*. Psychology Press.

129. Kenny, C., and Fraser, T. N. (2012). *Living Indigenous Leadership: Native Narratives on Building Strong Communities*. UBC Press.

130. Kenshalo, D. R. (2012). *Sensory Functions of the Skin of Humans*. Springer Science and Business Media.

131. Khanorkar, S. V. (2011). *Insights in Physiology*. JP Medical Ltd.

132. Kiernan, J., and Rajakumar, R. (2013). *Barr's The Human Nervous System: An Anatomical Viewpoint*. Lippincott Williams and Wilkins.

133. Kirov, B. (2014). *Mahatma Gandhi: Quotes and Facts*.

134. Kissin, B. (2012). *Conscious and Unconscious Programs in the Brain*. Springer Science and Business Media.

135. Koob, G. F., Arends, M. A., and Moal, M. L. (2014). *Drugs, Addiction, and the Brain*. Academic Press.

136. Kouzes, J. M., and Posner, B. Z. (2012). *The Leadership Challenge: How to Make Extraordinary Things Happen in Organizations*. John Wiley and Sons.

137. Kratz, R. F., and Siegfried, D. R. (2010). *Biology For Dummies*. John Wiley and Sons.

138. Kroc, R., and Anderson, R. (1992). *Grinding It Out: The Making Of McDonald's*. St. Martin's Press.

139. Kucia, J. F., and Gravett, L. S. (2014). *Leadership in Balance: New Habits of the Mind*. Palgrave Macmillan.

140. Kumari, V., Bob, P., and Boutros, N. (2014). *Electrophysiology and Psychophysiology in Psychiatry and Psychopharmacology*. Springer.

141. Lac, K. (2012). *Jeff Bezos (Founder and CEO of Amazon)*. Hyperink Inc.

142. Larsen, K. (2005). *Stephen Hawking: A Biography*. Greenwood Publishing Group.

143. Lehrer, P. M., Woolfolk, R. L., and Sime, W. E. (2007). *Principles and Practice of Stress Management, Third Edition*. Guilford Press.

144. Lesinski, J. M. (2009). *Bill Gates: Entrepreneur and Philanthropist*. Twenty-First Century Books.

145. *Life Stories of Authentic Leaders in Higher Education Administration*. (2007). ProQuest.

146. Linden, R. W. A. (1998). *The Scientific Basis of Eating: Taste and Smell, Salivation, Mastication and Swallowing, and Their Dysfunctions.* Karger Medical and Scientific Publishers.

147. Littel, M. (2006). *McDougal Littell World History: Patterns of Interaction: Reading Study Guide, English Grades 9-12.* Houghton Mifflin Harcourt (HMH).

148. Lovallo, W. R. (2015). *Stress and Health: Biological and Psychological Interactions.* SAGE Publications.

149. Lucas, G., and Kline, S. (1999). *George Lucas: Interviews.* Univ. Press of Mississippi.

150. Lu, L. C., and Bludau, J. (2011). *Alzheimer's Disease.* ABC-CLIO.

151. Lusted, M. A. (2011). *Mark Zuckerberg: Facebook Creator.* ABDO.

152. Malgonkar, M. (2008). *The Men Who Killed Gandhi.* Roli Books Private Limited.

153. Management, I. of L. and. (2012). *Planning to Work Efficiently.* Routledge.

154. Mancall, E. L., and Brock, D. G. (2011). *Gray's Clinical Neuroanatomy.* Elsevier Health Sciences.

155. Mangal, S. K. (2013). *General Psychology.* Sterling Publishers Pvt. Ltd.

156. Mann, J., and Truswell, S. (2012). *Essentials of Human Nutrition.* OUP Oxford.

157. Marcus, D. (2009). *Chronic Pain: A Primary Care Guide to Practical Management.* Springer Science and Business Media.

158. Marcus, E. M., and Jacobson, S. (2012). *Integrated Neuroscience: A Clinical Problem Solving Approach.* Springer Science and Business Media.

159. Marques, J. (2014). *Leadership and Mindful Behavior: Action, Wakefulness, and Business.* Palgrave Macmillan.

160. Marshall, P. (1991). *Awakenings.*

161. Martinez, J. (2013). *Carlos Slim: The Richest Man in the World/the Authorized Biography.* Titletown Publishing, LLC.

162. Martin, G. N. (2013). *The Neuropsychology of Smell and Taste.* Taylor and Francis Group.

163. Maxwell, J. C. (2007). *The 21 Indispensable Qualities of a Leader: Becoming the Person Others Will Want to Follow.* Thomas Nelson Inc.

164. McAnulty, R. D., and Burnette, M. M. (2006). *Sex and Sexuality: Sexual function and dysfunction.* Greenwood Publishing Group.

165. McConnell, J. V. (1983). *Understanding human behavior: an introduction to psychology.* Holt, Rinehart and Winston.

166. McGuigan, F. J. (1987). *Critical Issues in Psychology, Psychiatry, and Physiology: A Memorial to W. Horsley Gantt.* Taylor and Francis.

167. McKenzie, J. S. (2013). *The Basal Ganglia: Structure and Function.* Springer Science and Business Media.

168. M.D, S. S. P. (2010). *Your Brain and Business: The Neuroscience of Great Leaders.* FT Press.

169. Media, A. (2012). *Ear Infections: A troubleshooting guide to common childhood ailments.* Adams Media.

170. Menini, A. (2009). *The Neurobiology of Olfaction.* CRC Press.

171. Metz, R. F. (2011). *Coaching in the Library: A Management Strategy for Achieving Excellence.* American Library Association.

172. Miller, B. L., and Cummings, J. L. (2007). *The Human Frontal Lobes: Functions and Disorders.* Guilford Press.

173. Miller, F. P., Vandome, A. F., and McBrewster, J. (2011). *Joe Jamail.* VDM Publishing.

174. Møller, A. R., Langguth, B., DeRidder, D., and Kleinjung, T. (2010). *Textbook of Tinnitus.* Springer Science and Business Media.

175. Moller, A. R., Langguth, B., Hajak, G., Kleinjung, T., and Cacace, A. (2007). *Tinnitus: Pathophysiology and Treatment.* Elsevier.

176. Montgomery, S., and Grandin, T. (2012). *Temple Grandin: How the Girl Who Loved Cows Embraced Autism and Changed the World.* Houghton Mifflin Harcourt.

177. Morgan, J., and Bloom, O. (2006). *Cells of the Nervous System.* Infobase Publishing.

178. Mouritsen, O. G., and Styrb¾k, K. (2014). *Umami: Unlocking the Secrets of the Fifth Taste.* Columbia University Press.

179. Moxley, R. S. (2015). *Becoming a Leader Is Becoming Yourself.* McFarland.

180. Mucignat-Caretta, C. (2014). *Neurobiology of Chemical Communication.* CRC Press.

181. Nevid, J. S. (2014). *Essentials of Psychology: Concepts and Applications.* Cengage Learning.

182. Nomura, Y. (2013). *Morphological Aspects of Inner Ear Disease.* Springer Science and Business Media.

183. Noyd, R. K., Krueger, J. A., and Hill, K. M. (2016). *Biology: Organisms and Adaptations, Media Update, Enhanced Edition.* Cengage Learning.

184. O'Connor, R. (2015). *Rewire: Change Your Brain to Break Bad Habits, Overcome Addictions, Conquer Self-destructive Behavior.* Penguin Group USA.

185. Olver, K. (2008). *Empowered Leadership eBook.* Kim Olver.

186. Ostafin, B. D., Robinson, M. D., and Meier, B. P. (2015). *Handbook of Mindfulness and Self-Regulation.* Springer.

187. Ovalle, W. K., and Nahirney, P. C. (2013). *Netter's Essential Histology.* Elsevier Health Sciences.

188. Palcy, E. (1998). *Ruby Bridges.*

189. Pastorino, E. E., and Doyle-Portillo, S. M. (2012). *Cengage Advantage Books: What is Psychology? Essentials.* Cengage Learning.

190. Pepe, T., and Consulting, N. K. (2000). *So, What's All the Sniff About?: An In-Depth Plea for Sanity and Equal Rights for Your Sense*

of Smell, Our Most Neglected and Endangered Sense. So Whats all the Sniff about.

191. Perot, R. (1996). *Ross Perot: My Life and the Principles for Success.* Summit Publishing Group.

192. Perry, E. K., Ashton, H., and Young, A. H. (2002). *Neurochemistry of Consciousness: Neurotransmitters in Mind.* John Benjamins Publishing.

193. Pickles, J. O. (2012). *An Introduction to the Physiology of Hearing.* BRILL.

194. Porter-O'Grady, T., and Malloch, K. (2010). *Innovation Leadership: Creating the Landscape of Healthcare.* Jones and Bartlett Learning.

195. Porter, S. (2013). *Tidy's Physiotherapy.* Elsevier Health Sciences.

196. Pringle, P. (2008). *Top 10 Qualities of a Great Leader.* Harrison House Publishers.

197. Puri, S. A., Amma, and Devi, S. M. A. (2014). *The Color Of The Rainbow.* M A Center.

198. Rassool, G. H. (2011). *Understanding Addiction Behaviours: Theoretical and Clinical Practice in Health and Social Care.* Palgrave Macmillan.

199. Rathus, S. A. (2006). *Psychology: Concepts and Connections.* Cengage Learning.

200. Rensburg, L. J. van. (2012). *Study Secrets of a Straight 'A' Student.* Lulu.com.

201. Reynolds, M. D. (1991). *Women champions of human rights: eleven U.S. leaders of the twentieth century.* McFarland.

202. Rhoades, R., and Bell, D. R. (2009). *Medical Physiology: Principles for Clinical Medicine.* Lippincott Williams and Wilkins.

203. Rhoads, J., and PhD, P. M. (2014). *Clinical Consult to Psychiatric Nursing for Advanced Practice.* Springer Publishing Company.

204. Riggio, R. E., Chaleff, I., and Lipman-Blumen, J. (2008). *The Art of Followership: How Great Followers Create Great Leaders and Organizations.* John Wiley and Sons.

205. Rosdahl, C. B., and Kowalski, M. T. (2008). *Textbook of Basic Nursing.* Lippincott Williams and Wilkins.

206. Rosenbaum, L. (1989). *Biofeedback frontiers: self-regulation of stress reactivity.* AMS Press.

207. Rubin, R. H., and Pfaff, D. W. (2010). *Hormone/Behavior Relations of Clinical Importance: Endocrine Systems Interacting with Brain and Behavior.* Academic Press.

208. Ruettiger, R. (2012). *Rudy: My Story.* Thomas Nelson Inc.

209. Running, C.A., Craig, B. A. and Mattes, R.D. (2015). *Oleogustus: The Unique Taste of Fat Oxford.* University Press.

210. Russell, J., and Cohn, R. (2012). *Michael Bloomberg.* Book on Demand.

211. Rybolt, T. R., and Rybolt, L. M. (2009). *Ace Your Science Project about the Senses: Great Science Fair Ideas.* Enslow Publishers, Inc.

212. Sachdev, P. S., and Keshavan, M. S. (2010). *Secondary Schizophrenia.* Cambridge University Press.

213. Saito, H. (1988). *Neurotransmitters as Modulators of Blood Pressure.* VSP.

214. Sanchez, F. (2008). *Almost O.K.: The Difference Between Life and Death - A Close Look at Suicide.* Xlibris Corporation.

215. Sanes, D. H., Reh, T. A., and Harris, W. A. (2011). *Development of the Nervous System.* Academic Press.

216. Schalkoff, R. J. (2011). *Intelligent Systems: Principles, Paradigms, and Pragmatics.* Jones and Bartlett Publishers.

217. Schalley, A. C., and Khlentzos, D. (2007). *Mental States: Language and cognitive structure.* John Benjamins Publishing.

218. Schopenhauer, A., and Runge, P. O. (2012). *On Vision and Colors; Color Sphere.* Chronicle Books.

219. Schultz, D. P., and Schultz, S. E. (2016). *Theories of Personality.* Cengage Learning.

220. Schwarzenegger, A. (2012). *Total Recall.* Simon and Schuster.

221. Scouller, J. (2011). *The Three Levels of Leadership: How to Develop Your Leadership Presence, Knowhow and Skill.* Management Books 2000.

222. Seka, M. I. (2014). *Life Lessons of Wisdom and Motivation - Volume II: Insightful, Enlightened and Inspirational quotations and proverbs.* Providential Press.

223. Selby, J. (2003). *Free Your Mind.* iUniverse.

224. Senior, C., Lee, N., and Braeutigam, S. (2015). *Society, Organizations and the Brain: building towards a unified cognitive neuroscience perspective.* Frontiers Media SA.

225. Sherrow, V. (1994). *Mohandas Gandhi.* Millbrook Press.

226. Shinghal, J. N. (2002). *Quick Bedside Prescriber.* B. Jain Publishers.

227. Siegel, A. (1999). *Open and Clothed: For the Passionate Clothes Lover.* Agapanthus Books.

228. Siegel, A., and Sapru, H. N. (2010). *Essential Neuroscience.* Lippincott Williams and Wilkins.

229. Singh, I. B. (2008). *Essentials of Anatomy.* Jaypee Brothers Publishers.

230. Smith, H. A., Blecha, M. K., and Sternig, J. (1966). *Science.* Laidlaw.

231. Smith, T., and Miller, A. (2014). *101 Tips for Parents of Children with Autism: Effective Solutions for Everyday Challenges.* Jessica Kingsley Publishers.

232. Snyder, S. (2013). *Leadership and the Art of Struggle: How Great Leaders Grow Through Challenge and Adversity.* Berrett-Koehler Publishers.

233. Sowards, J. K. (Ed.). (1995). *Makers of World History, Vol. 1, 2nd Edition* (2 Sub edition). New York: St Martins Press.

234. Stolk, J. M., U'Prichard, D. C., and Fuxe, K. (1988). *Epinephrine in the Central Nervous System.* Oxford University Press.

235. Szalma, D. J. L., and Hancock, P. P. A. (2012). *Performance Under Stress.* Ashgate Publishing, Ltd.

236. Talbott, S. M., and Kraemer, W. J. (2007). *The Cortisol Connection: Why Stress Makes You Fat and Ruins Your Health - And What You Can Do about It.* Hunter House.

237. Tarantino, Q. (1994). *Pulp Fiction.*

238. *The Practitioner.* (1992). John Brigg.

239. *The Story of the Weeping Camel.* (2002). Fox.

240. Thompson, R. F. (1975). *Introduction to physiological psychology.* Harper and Row Limited.

241. Tresilian, J. (2012). *Sensorimotor Control and Learning: An Introduction to the Behavioral Neuroscience of Action.* Palgrave Macmillan.

242. Wagner, H., and Silber, K. (2004). *Instant Notes in Physiological Psychology.* Taylor and Francis.

243. Walsh, C. T., and Schwartz-Bloom, R. D. (2004). *Pharmacology: Drug Actions and Reactions.* CRC Press.

244. Weiner, I. B. (2003). *Handbook of Psychology, Biological Psychology.* John Wiley and Sons.

245. Weisinger, H., and Pawliw-Fry, J. P. (2015). *Performing Under Pressure: The Science of Doing Your Best When It Matters Most.* Crown Publishing Group.

246. Wied, D. de, and Keep, P. A. van. (2012). *Hormones and the Brain.* Springer Science and Business Media.

247. Williams-Boyd, P. (2002). *Educational Leadership: A Reference Handbook.* ABC-CLIO.

248. Williams, P., and Denney, J. (2010). *The Leadership Wisdom of Solomon: 28 Essential Strategies for Leading with Integrity.* Standard Publishing.

249. Wiseman, L., and McKeown, G. (2010). *Multipliers: How the Best Leaders Make Everyone Smarter.* Harper Collins.

250. Wright, D. B. (2000). *Human Physiology and Health.* Heinemann.

251. Yeoman, I., McMahon-Beattie, U., Fields, K., Meethan, K., and Albrecht, J. (2015). *The Future of Food Tourism: Foodies, Experiences, Exclusivity, Visions and Political Capital.* Channel View Publications.

252. Zhaoping, L., and Li, Z. (2014). *Understanding Vision: Theory, Models, and Data.* Oxford University Press.

253. Zillmer, E. A., Spiers, M. V., and Culbertson, W. (2007). *Principles of Neuropsychology.* Cengage Learning.

WEBSITE REFERENCES

1. Idsiach. (2006). Idsiach. Retrieved 7 February, 2016, from http:// people.idsia.ch/~juergen/einstein.html

2. Upfromsplatcom. (2010). Upfromsplatcom. Retrieved 7 February, 2016, from http://upfromsplat.com/cynthia-stafford-win-lottery/

3. Eric Evans. (2011). Bbccouk. Retrieved 7 February, 2016, from http://www.bbc.co.uk/history/british/victorians/overview_ victorians_01.shtml

4. Mo Costandi. (2006). The philosophy of "The Matrix." Retrieved 7 February, 2016, from https://neurophilosophy.wordpress. com/2006/12/11/the-philosophy-of-the-matrix/

5. Brownedu. (2000). Brownedu. Retrieved 8 February, 2016, from http://www.cog.brown.edu/courses/cg0001/lectures/ visualpaths.html

6. James Clear. (2016). Jamesclearcom. Retrieved 8 February, 2016, from http://jamesclear.com/implementation-intentions

7. Eddie Harmon-Jones . (2009). Psychology Today. Retrieved 8 February, 2016, from https://www.psychologytoday.com/blog/ the-social-emotional-brain/200904/unplugging-the-computer-metaphor

8. Girlscoutsorg. (2016). Girl Scouts of the USA. Retrieved 8 February, 2016, from http://www.girlscouts.org/en/cookies/all-about-cookies/Cookie-History.html

REFERENCED LEADER'S SOURCES AND ADDITIONAL INFORMATION

Page 15

Chris Gardner was a homeless father with a toddler in tow (1980's) who became a stockbroker millionaire, author, and producer of his own story.

» https://en.wikipedia.org/wiki/Chris_Gardner

» http://www.chrisgardnermedia.com/chris-gardner-biography. html

Albert Einstein 1879-1955 with an estimated I.Q. of 160 developed the general theory of relativity— a pillar of modern physics-- and is a historically renowned scientist that used his intellect to change the course of history.

» https://en.wikipedia.org/wiki/Albert_Einstein

» http://www.cse.emory.edu/sciencenet/mismeasure/genius/re-search04.html

Cynthia Stafford was a struggling mom caring for five children when she won 112 Million dollars in 2007 and became known as one of Los Angeles' biggest philanthropists.

» https://www.youtube.com/watch?v=r_lcvBfLLoQ

» http://www.huffingtonpost.com/andrea-chalupa/how-to-win-the-lottery_b_206570.html

» http://www.blackgivesback.com/2011/06/philanthropist-cynthia-stafford-hosts.html#.VsGCD8c5nIM

In the early 1980's a confident Tony Robbins claimed he could correct a stranger's phobia within minutes on live Radio, Stage and TV, then did.

» http://www.cnn.com/TRANSCRIPTS/1007/30/lkl.01.html

British monarch Queen Victoria 1837-1901 lent her name to The Victorian Era and increased the size (**see size increase below**) of her kingdom many fold during her exceptionally long reign (**Specifically, 63 years and seven months**).

» http://www.royal.gov.uk/historyofthemonarchy/kingsandqueensoftheunitedkingdom/thehanoverians/victoria.aspx

» https://en.wikipedia.org/wiki/Queen_Victoria#Legacy

» http://www.biography.com/people/queen-victoria-9518355#early-life

(**Size increase: "During her reign, Britain expanded its imperial reach, doubling in size and encompassing Canada, Australia, India and various possessions in Africa and the South Pacific."**)

Page 16

[...] introverted peace revolutionaries like Mahatma Gandhi who despite his self-reflective nature was the political Leader of the Indian independence movement in the 1940's.

» https://en.wikipedia.org/wiki/Mahatma_Gandhi

» http://www.quietrev.com/gandhi-on-the-value-of-introversion/

> » http://www.biography.com/people/mahatma-gandhi-9305898#spiritual-and-political-leader
>
> » https://simple.wikipedia.org/wiki/Indian_independence_movement

Henry Ford who in the late 1800's **(Correction: early 1900's, not 1800's)** optimized automobile production with the installation of assembly lines

> » http://www.history.com/this-day-in-history/fords-assembly-line-starts-rolling
>
> » http://www.biography.com/people/henry-ford-9298747#ford-motor-company
>
> » https://en.wikipedia.org/wiki/Assembly_line

("Ransom Olds patented the assembly line concept, which he put to work in his Olds Motor Vehicle Company factory in 1901.[10] This development is often overshadowed by Henry Ford, who perfected the assembly line by installing driven conveyor belts that could produce a Model T in 93 minutes.[9] The assembly line developed for the Ford Model T began operation on December 1, 1913.)

Quote:

According to Steve Jobs – unarguably a leader – "Picasso had a saying –'Good Artists Copy; Great Artists Steal" https://www.youtube.com/watch?v=CWODUg63lqU

> » http://www.cnet.com/news/what-steve-jobs-really-meant-when-he-said-good-artists-copy-great-artists-steal/

Actual quote by Jobs: "Picasso had a saying -- 'good artists copy; great artists steal' has often been misquoted as "Good Artists Copy; Great Artists Steal"

> » http://quoteinvestigator.com/2013/03/06/artists-steal/

("In 1892 an important precursor of this family of expressions was published. The author was W. H. Davenport Adams, and his words may have influenced the version that T. S. Eliot published in 1920. Both writers referenced "poets", but by 1959 a version with "artists" was in circulation. The expression continued to metamorphose and instances were attributed to major artists such as Igor Stravinsky, William Faulkner, and Pablo Picasso. The attachment to Stravinsky depends on the credibility of Yates. QI has not yet located substantive evidence for the attribution to Picasso".)

Page 17

One February day in 1914 Rosa Parks sat on a bus and refused to move even though a white woman wanted her seat. The response to her refusal and the actions of the people around her, including others who had similarly refused to give up their seats, led to a boycott (**Specifically, Montgomery Bus Boycott**) that helped bring about the end of segregation in the public facilities of America.

» https://en.wikipedia.org/wiki/Rosa_Parks

» http://www.biography.com/people/rosa-parks-9433715#related-video-gallery

» http://www.history.com/topics/black-history/civil-rights-movement

Page 17

Quote:

"Happiness Is When, What You Think, What You Say, And What You Do Are In Harmony." ~Mahatma Gandhi

» https://en.wikiquote.org/wiki/Happiness

» http://www.brainyquote.com/quotes/quotes/m/mahatmagan105593.html

Page 18

Quote:

"Whether You Think You Can, Or You Think You Can't – You're Right." ~Henry Ford

» http://www.forbes.com/sites/erikaandersen/2013/05/31/21-quotes-from-henry-ford-on-business-leadership-and-life/#5be8e03c3700

» http://www.biography.com/people/henry-ford-9298747#synopsis

Page 22

Quote:

William Shakespeare coined the phrase, "Some are born great, some achieve greatness, and some have greatness thrust upon them," in the early 1600's. This line from the play "Twelfth Night" was so intrinsically resonant with humans that it is even entrenched in popular speech today. It has evolved as a saying reinforcing the possibility of changing your destiny.

» http://nfs.sparknotes.com/twelfthnight/page_110.html

» https://en.wikipedia.org/wiki/Malvolio

» https://en.wikipedia.org/wiki/Twelfth_Night

Page 25-28

Oskar Schindler (1908-1974) [...] He is the subject of the Steven Spielberg movie Schindler's List with Liam Neeson and was a German industrialist spy, a member of the Nazi party, who amassed a fortune by using Jews for cheap labor and then spent it all to save the very race he was exploiting. Schindler's List refers to the names of the 1,200 Jews he saved during the Holocaust. Oskar Schindler is an apparent enigma and has been labeled opportunist by many. His story is littered with risky business, some successes, more failures, wives, mistresses, legitimate as well as illegitimate offspring, subterfuge and danger. Schindler himself estimated his wartime (1942-1945) acquisitions and expenditures (including bribes and relocations costs) related to saving Jews at $1,056,000 (a huge amount of money for that period). He ended the war destitute.

[...] was even arrested three times

Schindler often dressed up for the role and played out the subterfuge.

From the child who forged school documents to the husband living off rich in laws and impregnating a mistress while driving businesses into bankruptcy

[...] once the war ended he couldn't figure out how to build richness and purpose in the day-to-day dun drum of typical business planning. Perhaps that is also why, after yet another bankruptcy, he left his wife and went back to Germany to get closer to the history of his success and to reclaim a FEELing of purpose.

So his return to Germany resulted in even more failed businesses and the closest he came to his own Greatness was the Jewish gratitude money that kept him alive over the years.

» http://www.jewishvirtuallibrary.org/jsource/biography/schindler.html

» https://en.wikipedia.org/wiki/Oskar_Schindler

» (Crowe, David M. (2004). Oskar Schindler: The Untold Account of His Life, Wartime Activities, and the True Story Behind the List. Cambridge, MA: Westview Press.ISBN 978-0-465-00253-5)

» Steinhouse, Herbert (April 1994). "The Real Oskar Schindler". Saturday Night (Andela Publishing). Retrieved 28 June 2013.

» Roberts, Jack L. (1996). The Importance of Oskar Schindler. The Importance Of biography series. San Diego: Lucent. ISBN 1-56006-079-4.

» Thompson, Bruce, ed. (2002). Oskar Schindler. People Who Made History. San Diego: Greenhaven Press. ISBN 0-7377-0894-8.

REFERENCED LEADER'S SOURCES and ADDITIONAL INFORMATION

» http://www.ushmm.org/wlc/en/article.php?ModuleId=10005787

Quote:

"Reality Is An Illusion: Albeit A Very Persistent One." ~Albert Einstein

» http://www.quotationspage.com/quote/26844.html
» http://www.brainyquote.com/quotes/quotes/a/al-berteins100298.html

Page 30-32

Mary Temple Grandin PhD (1947~) was diagnosed with autism as a preschooler. She is known for changing an entire industry's approach to the inhumane treatment of cattle because, in some ways, she thinks like a cow. She is also known for enlightening parents and teachers on the subject of autism. Her early life and academic career were steered by the unusual nature of her brain's processing. She was slow to speak, socially challenged, repetitious in her behaviors and copying skills.

Dr. Grandin herself was referred to as a tape recorder and teased at school for this form of echoing. With a desire to understand her differences from the cellular level Temple Grandin underwent testing using modern imaging techniques. Diffusion Tensor Imaging, a method that traces connections between brain regions, made her challenged neuronal connections visible. Additionally via magnetic resonance, an imaging technique that looks at structure, her oversized amygdala and undersized facial recognition software areas were pictured.

Dr. Grandin attributes this affinity for understanding the mind of the cow, to visualization patterns caused by her autism. She has been reported to say that these skills have taught her to comprehend how changes in visual details can cause changes in sensory sensitivity in cattle. This connection led her to design humane animal handling equipment that strongly influenced the way cattle are treated while being prepared for slaughter.

Mary Temple Grandin is a highly educated award winning Dr./ speaker, prolific author respected scientist at the forefront of animal activism and autism education. She has brought great insight to the parents and educators of autism. She is the inventor of the Hug Box, inspired by noting that since cattle calmed in a squeeze box she might be able to calm her own anxiety in a similar fashion, she adapted the design for use with humans. Dr. Grandin is a famous Leader with autism and has stated that there is no cure; she will always be autistic.

» http://www.grandin.com
» https://en.wikipedia.org/wiki/Temple_Grandin
» *Mayo Clinic staff.* "Language development: Speech milestones for babies". Retrieved 19 January 2014.
» 'Temple Grandin Inducted into Colorado Women's Hall of Fame',http://www.wherefoodcomesfrom.com/article/2281/Temple-Grandin-Inducted-into-Colorado-Womens-Hall-of-Fame#. UdA8G2thiK0, retrieved 30 June 2013.
» The Way I See It: A Personal Look at ... – Temple Grandin – Google Books. *Books.google.com.* Retrieved 2011-11-17.
» http://www.nytimes.com/1997/08/05/science/qualities-of-an-animal-scientist-cow-s-eye-view-and-autism.html?pagewanted=all
» http://discovermagazine.com/2013/april/2-exploring-temple-grandins-brain

Quote:
"As You Think, So Shall You Be." ~ Wayne W. Dyer
» http://www.famous-quotes.com/author.php?aid=2188
» http://thinkexist.com/quotation/as_you_think_so_shall_you_be-since_you_cannot/298461.html

Page 34-36

Daniel Ruettiger (1948~), more commonly known as "RUDY"

...RUDY is the real life character made famous in the film RUDY. Thus the film story is the one most known: RUDY who was the third child in a family of sixteen **(fourteen children two parents)**, had a dream to play football for Notre Dame, and did. RUDY was dyslexic and his grades were too low for Notre Dame. However after many side routes and four application attempts, his hard work, persistence, definition of purpose and the absolute belief that he could make it happen paid off. RUDY managed to get accepted to the University.

However, getting onto the football team required even more steadfast hard work and persistence. RUDY had many hurdles. For example, to name just a few, he was small 5'6" 165 lbs, and had a lack of natural skill. Despite the impediments RUDY managed to be placed on the practice team. His absolute passion and fortitude were so admirable that eventually- on the last game of his senior year- RUDY was dressed and asked to get on the field.

Despite RUDY's lack of scored points or importance to the actual plays of the game itself, RUDY was an inspiration to the players and became one of only two Notre Dame players ever to be carried from the field.

Leading [athletes] to dig deep and "work harder" eventually culminating in the High School Football "Rudy" Awards in search of recipients that personify the "Four C's of Courage, Character, Commitment and Contribution."

Rudy shopped this movie idea all over Hollywood as a nobody. Getting it made was against all odds. But he did it.

» https://en.wikipedia.org/wiki/Rudy_Ruettiger
» Rudy Chasing the Frog. Chasingthefrog.com (1971-02-25). Retrieved on 2012-04-19.

REFERENCED LEADER'S SOURCES and ADDITIONAL INFORMATION

» Dick Weiss, SLIGHTING IRISH HURTS ALLEGED USC TAUNTS INSPIRE NOTRE DAME

Quote:

"We are what we repeatedly do. Excellence, then, is not an act but a habit."

- Will Durant (not Aristotle to whom this quote is often attributed)

» http://blogs.umb.edu/quoteunquote/2012/05/08/its-a-much-more-effective-quotation-to-attribute-it-to-aristotle-rather-than-to-will-durant/

» http://shimercollege.wikia.com/wiki/Fake_Quotes_Project/Aristotle/We_are_what_we_repeatedly_do

Page 50-52

Helen Adams Keller (1880-1968) and Johanna Anne Mansfield Sullivan Macy (1866-1936)...

Both women lost their sight as children due to illness. Helen Keller, however, was younger, more of an infant at the time, and lost her hearing as well. When Helen was eight years old and Anne was twenty the two met...

...their tale has been made into a movie many times over.

Their Story (in all likelihood and according to today's science): Helen was nearly without communication when Anne, whose sight had been marginally restored via surgery, arrived to teach Helen sign language. Anne's ability to teach and reach the non-communicative Helen was challenged by many things, most notably the fact that Helen didn't even comprehend the concept that every object had a name. After many struggles and with great persistence Anne managed to enlighten Helen and bring a vision of things into her mind via language. She did this by touching the object and then performing signs on Helen's hand. After that Helen was a voracious learner who eventually managed speech. She traveled, speaking, winning awards, writing articles, writing books and being a friend to powerful people.

When Helen was unaware of object naming, no conceptual understanding of her world could be formed and passed to others in order to be built upon and passed back again. Anne had begun the teaching with pre-decided lists of signed words but quickly noticed that Helen was not responding to these. She adapted her style and switched to words based upon Helen's interests. This new understanding added to Anne's vision of her blind/deaf student who blossomed before her from challenged student to brilliant girl.

» https://en.wikipedia.org/wiki/Anne_Sullivan

» McGinnity, B.L, J Seymour-Ford, and K.J Andries. "Anne Sullivan." Perkins School for the Blind. February 14, 2014. Accessed February 14, 2014.

» http://www.perkins.org/vision-loss/helen-keller/sullivan.html.

» http://www.perkins.org/history/people/helen-keller

Page 53

"Some men see things as they are and say why. I dream things that never were and say why not"." ~George Bernard Shaw

» http://www.bartleby.com/73/465.html

» https://books.google.com/books?id=91IFAYFh-tOMC&pg=PA93&lpg=PA93&dq="Some+men+-see+things+as+they+are+and+say+why.+I+dream+th-ings+that+never+were+and+say+why+not%22."++~George+Ber-nard+Shaw&source=bl&ots=phicC4RfEg&sig=nUK-V-Ca-jDP4l6zjKjpC0lLZr2Y&hl=en&sa=X&ved=0ahUKEwjAw-JvZ-pnLAhVW4WMKHYYUC7wQ6AEITjAI#v=onep-age&q="Some%20men%20see%20things%20as%20they%20

are%20and%20say%20why.%20I%20dream%20things%20
that%20never%20were%20and%20say%20why%20not%22."%20
%20~George%20Bernard%20Shaw&f=false

Page 66-68

Dr. Richard Alpert (1931-) renamed Ram Dass (1967) is the author of the culturally influential book "Be Here Now". The name Ram Dass means servant of God? And was given to him in India by Maharaji- a hindu guru and mystic. Ram Dass and Timothy Leary- a writer and psychologist known for advocating psychedelic drugs- were Harvard professors who researched and personally experimented with psychedelics.

These forays into the mentally distorting world of LSD purportedly introduced the Jewish born atheist doctor to God. Both Leary and Dass (then Dr. Alpert) were dismissed from Harvard in 1963 under controversial circumstances. Shortly thereafter Dass travelled to India where he met Maharaji.

The book "Be Here Now" was a huge success which brought the title phrase into common use. "Be Here Now" so influenced the American hippie generation that it is referred to as a "counterculture bible" and "seminal" to the era.

The book comes in four sections. 1- autobiographical quest from doctor to spiritually evolving as a yogi 2- metaphysical teachings 3- a manual or cookbook for "how to start down a spiritual path" 4- suggested readings. (**This is a summary in my own words – from sections of the book:**

> » "Journey: The Transformation: Dr. Richard Alpert, PhD. into Baba Ram Dass"
>
> » "From Bindu to Ojas: The Core Book"
>
> » "Cookbook for a Sacred Life: A Manual for Conscious Being"

» "Painted Cakes (Do Not Satisfy Hunger): Books")

» https://www.ramdass.org/bio/

» https://en.wikipedia.org/wiki/Ram_Dass

» *Starr, Bernard (July 19, 2007).* "Rite of passage: Turn-on or turn-off?". *Religion and Spirituality.com.* Retrieved November 23, 2011.

» "Baba Ram Dass". *Ramparts* **11**: 38. *He was, at this time, an atheist, and had difficulty even pronouncing 'spiritual'.*

» *Davidson, Sara (Fall 2006).* "The Ultimate Trip". Tufts Magazine. RetrievedNovember 23, 2011.

» "Biography: Richard Alpert/Ram Dass". *Ramdass.org. Ram Dass / Love Remember Serve Foundation.* Retrieved July 1, 2013.

» *Russin, Joseph M.; Weil, Andrew T. (May 28, 1963).* "The Crimson takes Leary, Alpert to Task: 'Roles' & 'Games' In William James". *The Harvard Crimson.* Retrieved August 8, 2011.

» https://en.wikipedia.org/wiki/Be_Here_Now_(book)

  » *Tempo staff (July 19, 2010).* "'Be Here Now' turns 40". *The Taos News.* Retrieved August 5, 2011.

  » *Garner, Dwight (January 8, 2010).* "Tune In, Turn On, Turn Page". *The New York Times.*

  » *Harvey, Andrew; Erickson, Karuna (2010). Heart Yoga: The Sacred Marriage of Yoga and Mysticism. North Atlantic Books.* ISBN 978-1-58394-291-8.

Page 69

Quote:

Be sure to put your feet in the right place, then stand firm. ~ Abraham Lincoln

» http://www.goodreads.com/quotes/24884-be-sure-you-put-your-feet-in-the-right-place

» http://www.mrlincolnswhitehouse.org/inside.asp?ID=65&sub-jectID=2

Page 81-82

Girl Scouts of the United States and Girl Guide's of Canada sell cookies as one of their primary means for fundraising. Originally founded in the UK by Robert Baden-Powel the founder of Scouting in 1907, (**"In 1907, he held the first Brownsea Island Scout camp, which is now seen as the beginning of Scouting" Powell founded scouting (mainly for boys) in the UK originally, but Juliette Gordon Low founded the Girl Scouts, specificially, in the US in 1912).**

The World Association of Girl Guides and Girl Scouts has grown into the largest voluntary movement dedicated to women and girls in the world. They represent ten million women and girls from 146 countries around the world. And though not every participating Girl Guide/Scout country sells cookies, and though the cookie recipes are quite varied, Girl Scout Cookies are internationally famous and have estimated annual sales worth $800 million in the USA alone.

For example, in Canada the birth of the cookie is attributed to a Leader in Regina, Saskatchewan who baked and packaged the first cookies as a means of raising money for camping equipment and uniforms. This story dates back to 1927 and is nationally recognized as true. However, in 1917 the Mistletoe Troop from Muskogee, OK stopped kissing for money and started selling sugar cookies instead. According to the American history of cookies these were the original Girl Guide cookies. In Singapore the great cookie sale was launched in 1994 and no one tries to say they came up with the cookie concept.

» https://en.wikipedia.org/wiki/Girl_Scouts_of_the_USA

» https://www.girlguides.ca/web/GGC/Default.aspx?hkey=f-6cbd051-db58-4e5d-9cc8-a732f8b05586&WebsiteKey=eaa3528e-7748-497f-96cd-a4c39f08750d

» http://www.girlscouts.org/

» http://mentalfloss.com/article/31222/numbers-how-americans-spend-their-money

» http://pabook2.libraries.psu.edu/palitmap/GirlScoutCookies.html

» http://www.girlguides.org.sg/ggs/slot/u48/history/Chronological%20View.pdf

Page 90

Quote:

"The way to entice people into cooking is to cook delicious things."~Yotam Ottolenghi

» https://quotesgram.com/yotam-ottolenghi-quotes/

» https://twitter.com/ottolenghi

» http://likesuccess.com/author/yotam-ottolenghi

Page 98-99

Ruby Bridges was a 6-year old African American girl who in 1960 helped to integrate the all-white schools of New Orleans. Although she was a young child she braved the faces of angry white citizens yelling and screaming at her while keeping their children away from her contamination every day. She was the only black girl to come to that school and because a black girl was in school the other moms kept their children away. So she was the only student, period. She was escorted to and from to keep her safe. Despite the cruel words of the white people that stood outside the school every morning and afternoon, she faced them with compassion and emerged unscathed, physically or emotionally. A white teacher from the North named Barbara Henry, helped and encouraged her. Her teacher, her mother, Lucille, and her own quiet strength, eventually broke down a century-old barrier forever, a pivotal moment in the civil-rights movement. This true story was made into a movie in 1998.

"And so I learned that a family and a child under great stress and fear could show exquisite dignity and courage because of their moral and religious values, and because they had a definite purpose in what they were trying to accomplish. This purpose made them resilient. I couldn't figure out the source of this resilience because I had only worked with well to do children who had nothing to work hard for, no reason pushing them to accomplish anything. So now I see that the issue is not stress but stress for what purpose? Having something to believe in protected Ruby from psychiatric symptoms and gave her a dignity and a strength that is utterly remarkable."

- » https://en.wikipedia.org/wiki/Ruby_Bridges
- » http://www.biography.com/people/ruby-bridges-475426#ostra-cized-at-school

"Ruby was the only student in Henry's class, because parents pulled or threatened to pull their children from Ruby's class and send them to other schools. For a full year, Henry and Ruby sat side by side at two desks, working on Ruby's lessons."

- » http://songbird1471.blogspot.com/2012/03/ruby-bridges-inspir-ing-story.html
- » http://www.cbn.com/special/blackhistory/undergod_rubybridg-es.aspx

Page 103

"Until you walk a mile in another man's moccasins you can't imagine the smell." ~Robert Byrne

- » http://www.quotes.net/quote/5222
- » http://www.quotationspage.com/quotes/Robert_Byrne/
- » http://www.qotd.org/search/search.html?aid=5847&page=3

Page 115-117

Mahatma Gandhi 1869-1948, was a lawyer and spiritual Leader who advocated for the civil rights of Indians, both at home under British rule and in South Africa. After the outbreak of World War I he moved from London and returned to India. He rejected his lawyer's suit; donned a loincloth and shawl, choosing to live the austere life of a spiritual Leader. He became known as "great soul" aka Mahatma. However in 1919 he mingled spirituality with politics by calling for peaceful protests in response to the Rowlatt Act, which allowed the British to imprison suspects without trial. His attempts at peaceful protestation were met with violence instead. The British killed approximately 400 people by opening fire on unarmed demonstrators. Gandhi spent the next 29 years leading peaceful protests, living in and out of prison; fasting as a means of getting countrymen cooperation. Gandhi led the Indian National Congress and advocated a policy of non-violence and non-cooperation to achieve home rule. In 1930, in one of his more notable adventures, Gandhi protested the Salt Acts - which prohibited Indians from collecting or selling salt – by walking in a loin cloth and shawl to the coastal town of Dandi (a 24 day trek) where he had gathered a crowd. He then broke the law by making salt from evaporated seawater. That year Gandhi and 60,000 Indians went to jail for similar acts.

Over the years Gandhi went in and out of prison often accompanied by his wife for acts of nonviolent noncompliance. After he launched the "Quit India" movement, meant to pressure The British into withdrawing from Indian Rule, he was again jailed. This time (1944) his wife died in his arms during their incarceration. Gandhi wanted a unified India but during independence negotiations of 1945 it became obvious he would not prevail and that there would be a partition of the subcontinent, along religious lines, creating two independent states Hindu (mostly Indian) and Muslim (mostly Pakistan). Violence between the Hindus and Muslims erupted. Gandhi went on another hunger strike to end the discord. However, his desire to unite the religious peoples caused hatred and feelings of betrayal by some Hindus. In 1948 Gandhi now 78 left his home to pray and was shot at point blank range by a Muslim who first knelt at Mahatma's feet. Godse, the killer, was executed for committing such a violent act.

» https://en.wikipedia.org/wiki/Mahatma_Gandhi

» *McGregor, Ronald Stuart (1993). The Oxford Hindi-English Dictionary. Oxford University Press. p. 799. ISBN 978-0-19-864339-5. Retrieved 31 August 2013.*

» *Khan, Yasmin (2007). The Great Partition: The Making of India and Pakistan. Yale University Press. p. 1. ISBN 978-0-300-12078-3. Retrieved 1 September2013.*

» Brown (1991), p. 380

» *Cush, Denise; Robinson, Catherine; York, Michael (2008). Encyclopedia of Hinduism. Taylor & Francis. p. 544. ISBN 978-0-7007-1267-0.*

» Mary Elizabeth King, "Mohandas K, Gandhi and Martin Luther King, Jr.'s Bequest: Nonviolent Civil Resistance in a Globalized World" in *Lewis V. Baldwin and Paul R. Dekar (2013)*

» http://www.biography.com/people/mahatma-gandhi-9305898#spiritual-and-political-leader

» https://simple.wikipedia.org/wiki/Indian_independence_movement

» http://www.history.co.uk/biographies/mahatma-gandhi

Page 119

"It's often just enough to be with someone. I don't need to touch them. Not even talk. A feeling passes between you both. You're not alone." ~Marilyn Monroe

» http://m.imdb.com/name/nm0000054/quotes

» http://thinkexist.com/quotation/it-s_often_just_enough_to_be_with_someone-i_don-t/153730.html

» https://www.psychologytoday.com/blog/in-the-name-love/201405/why-lovers-touch-is-so-powerful

Page 139-140

Michael Rubens Bloomberg KBE (1942-) American business magnate and multi billionaire is the founder, CEO; owner of Bloomberg L.P. and was the 108th mayor of New York City for 12 years. Bloomberg was elected just weeks following the September 11 terrorist attacks on the trade towers. Due to his wealth he was able to run for this office without bending to lobby groups or vested interests. It is reported that he spent 650 million dollars of his own money on New York City during his time as mayor. **(this is a minimum estimate, but was likely much more.)** He also gave up the yearly 2.7 million dollar salary and went out of pocket on all expenses related to traveling with staff and security. Bloomberg's views are clearly stated and backed by millions of dollars. He works to shape legislation and has committed 600 million to anti-tobacco efforts globally as well as millions more to road safety efforts in Brazil, Vietnam, Egypt. Presently he has been reported as a man trying to create a coalition of Mayors Making a Difference countrywide.

» http://www.biography.com/people/michael-bloomberg-16466704

» http://www.nytimes.com/2013/12/30/nyregion/cost-of-being-mayor-650-million-if-hes-rich.html?_r=0

» **The $650 million minimum estimate is undoubtedly low. Up-to-date annual reports were not available for several Bloomberg-financed organizations and a wide range of expenses were impossible to firmly establish...**

» http://www.telegraph.co.uk/news/worldnews/northamerica/usa/10542304/Michael-Bloomberg-spent-650-million-of-own-money-as-New-York-mayor.html

» http://www.who.int/tobacco/mpower/bloomberg_philanthropies_annual_updateL_ltr_march_2013.pdf

» http://nymag.com/news/features/michael-bloomberg-2012-6/

» http://www.bloomberg.org/program/government-innovation/
cities-service/#overview

Page 148

"Once we accept our limits, we go beyond them." ~Albert Einstein
(possibly misattributed to: Albert Einstein or Brendan Francis)

» https://en.wikiquote.org/wiki/Talk:Pragmatism

» http://www.art-quotes.com/auth_search.php?authid=3568#.
VuNh35N95HQ

Page 150-154

For the most part it appears that many historically impressive people
like Thomas Edison, Benjamin Franklin, William Shakespeare, Abraham
Lincoln, John D Rockefeller did succeed without proper schooling and
were undereducated by today's standards. However, during these varied
time periods, leaving school at young ages was a typical occurrence.
For example, some of today's unarguably successful highly influential
Leaders like Warren Buffet, Howard Stern, Barack Obama, Donald
Trump, Rachel Maddow, are all degreed professionals. Billionaires like
Bill Gates, Steve Jobs and Mark Zuckerberg may be college dropouts
but they discovered their vision, their passion and peer network while
in college. Groundbreakers like George Lucas, Ross Perot and Arnold
Schwarzenegger, who all managed to complete college degrees, also
attained highly memorable Leadership success status.

» http://www.education-reform.net/dropouts.htm

» https://en.wikipedia.org/wiki/Warren_Buffett#cite_note-War-
ren_Buffett_Timeline-23

   » *"Warren Buffett Timeline". About Money. Retrieved 30 April 2015.*

- » https://en.wikipedia.org/wiki/Howard_Stern
  - » Stern 1993, p. 115.
- » https://en.wikipedia.org/wiki/Barack_Obama#cite_note-31
  - » Boss-Bicak, Shira (January 2005). "Barack Obama '83". *Columbia College Today*. ISSN 0572-7820. Retrieved October 1, 2006.
- » https://en.wikipedia.org/wiki/Donald_Trump#cite_note-29
  - » Strauss, Valerie (July 17, 2015). "Yes, Donald Trump really went to an Ivy League school". The Washington Post. Retrieved January 17, 2016.
- » https://en.wikipedia.org/wiki/Rachel_Maddow#cite_note-stan9-21
  - » Sheridan, Barrett (May–June 2008). "Making Airwaves: Broadcaster Rachel Maddow is succeeding at her goal of 'lefty rabblerousing'". *Stanford Magazine*.
- » http://content.time.com/time/specials/packages/completelist/0,29569,1988080,00.html
- » http://www.forbes.com/sites/johngreathouse/2012/06/05/business-tips-from-college-dropouts-zuckerberg-jobs-gates-dell-ellison-branson-and-disney/#65bf7ae97986
- » https://en.wikipedia.org/wiki/Arnold_Schwarzenegger#cite_note-27
  - » "Campus Connection: Superior list of famous alumni?". *Wisconsin State Journal*. November 11, 2009. Retrieved April 11, 2012.
- » https://en.wikipedia.org/wiki/George_Lucas
- » https://en.wikipedia.org/wiki/Ross_Perot#cite_note-junior-10

Page 152-153

Walt Disney left high school, lied about his age, eventually drove an ambulance covered in cartoons and found Mickey Mouse.

» https://en.wikipedia.org/wiki/Walt_Disney

» http://www.justdisney.com/walt_disney/timeline/

» http://www.waltdisney.org/blog/over-there-walt-disneys-world-war-i-adventure

» https://chicagoredcrossstories.wordpress.com/tag/walt-disney/

Ray Kroc, who turned McDonald's into the largest food chain, also quit school, lied about his age and drove an ambulance.

» http://www.biography.com/people/ray-kroc-9369349

» http://www.mcdonalds.com/us/en/our_story/our_history/the_ray_kroc_story.html

Like Richard Branson, the famous entrepreneurial dyslexic [...]

» http://understandingdyslexia.com/richard-branson.htm

» http://www.biography.com/people/richard-branson-9224520#early-life

Disney, Kroc and Branson dropped out of school. They saw things differently enough to land at the top of the 20 percent club.

But then the same is true of college graduates Oprah Winfrey and Steven Spielberg (who by the way took over 30 years to graduate). **(33 years after dropped out of college)**

» https://en.wikipedia.org/wiki/Oprah_Winfrey

» http://www.telegraph.co.uk/culture/film/3579578/Spielberg-why-I-went-back-to-college.html

Even actress Mayim Bialik from The Big Bang Theory would likely have been invited to play the part of a woman with a PhD even if she wasn't already one. https://en.wikipedia.org/wiki/Mayim_Bialik#cite_note-17

REFERENCED LEADER'S SOURCES and ADDITIONAL INFORMATION

» *"Biography". Mayim Bialik. Retrieved January 25, 2014.*

» http://edition.cnn.com/2011/HEALTH/07/15/mayim.bialik.big.bang.theory/

Page 153

Stephen Hawking, Jane Goodall, Carlos Slim, and Joe Jamail all required a high level degree to be the forces they are today.

» https://en.wikipedia.org/wiki/Stephen_Hawking

  » Ferguson 2011, p. 47.

» http://www.biography.com/people/stephen-hawking-9331710#early-life

» http://www.janegoodall.ca/goodall-bio-timeline.php

» https://en.wikipedia.org/wiki/Jane_Goodall

  » *"Curriculum Vitae, Jane Goodall, PhD, DBE" (PDF). Jane Goodall Institute. Archived from the original (PDF) on 26 April 2012. Retrieved 28 July 2010.*

» https://en.wikipedia.org/wiki/Carlos_Slim

  » "Carlos Slim Interview – page 3 / 9 – Academy of Achievement:". Academy of Achievement. Retrieved May 10, 2015.

» https://en.wikipedia.org/wiki/Joe_Jamail

"...Charles Dickens (quit school) or a Dr. Phil (finished school)."

» http://www.biography.com/people/charles-dickens-9274087#early-life'

» http://www.britannica.com/biography/Charles-Dickens-British-novelist

» http://www.drphil.com/shows/page/bio/

...uneducated celebrities like Al Pacino, John Travolta, Ryan Gosling, Johnny Depp, Hillary Swank, Seth Rogen, Eminem, Robert Downey Jr., Robert De Niro, Jim Carrey, Roseanne Barr, and the amazing Quentin Tarantino...

» http://www.businessinsider.com/celebrity-high-school-drop-outs-2014-1
» http://www.collegedropoutshalloffame.com/s.htm
» https://en.wikipedia.org/wiki/Al_Pacino
» http://www.biography.com/people/al-pacino-9431474#early-life
» https://en.wikipedia.org/wiki/John_Travolta
  » Reeves, Michael. "Travolta recalls lonely high schooldays", *The StarPhoenix*, September 28, 1978. Accessed June 12, 2011.
» http://www.biography.com/people/john-travolta-9509927#early-career
» https://en.wikipedia.org/wiki/Ryan_Gosling
  » Ryan Gosling". *People*. Retrieved January 26, 2012.
» http://www.biography.com/people/johnny-depp-9542522#early-life
» https://en.wikipedia.org/wiki/Hilary_Swank
» https://en.wikipedia.org/wiki/Seth_Rogen
  » Kaufman, Amy (March 14, 2011). "Judd Apatow's 'Freaks and Geeks' gang reminisces – and mocks James Franco". *Los Angeles Times* (Tribune Company). Retrieved June 16, 2011.
» http://www.biography.com/people/eminem-9542093#early-life
» http://www.biography.com/people/robert-downey-jr-9542052
» http://www.biography.com/people/robert-de-niro-9271729#early-life
» https://en.wikipedia.org/wiki/Charlie_Sheen
» http://www.imdb.com/name/nm0000120/bio

» http://roseanne.wikia.com/wiki/Roseanne_Barr

» https://en.wikipedia.org/wiki/Quentin_Tarantino

> *Giang, Vivian (May 20, 2013). "10 Wildly Successful People Who Dropped Out Of High School". Business Insider. Retrieved July 14, 2015.*

Page 165

Billionaire Jeff Bezos (1964~) – founder and CEO of Amazon.com-- is responsible for most of the 42 million dollars raised towards building The Clock of Long Now which is designed to run for 10,000 years and to be buried deep in the Sierra Diablo Mountains on Bezos' land. Bezos is an engineer and computer scientist with a mechanical genius and an eccentric taste for life. For example, Bezos has spent years attempting to privatize space travel and engages in unusual pastimes like recovering the engines from the famed Apollo 11, which he found on the bottom of the Atlantic Ocean.

» https://en.wikipedia.org/wiki/Jeff_Bezos

» https://www.princeton.edu/engineering/news/archive/?tag=-jeff-bezos

» http://www.dailymail.co.uk/sciencetech/article-2296535/Has-Amazon-billionaire-Jeff-Bezos-recovered-rockets-launched-Apollo-11s-historic-1969-mission-moon.html

» http://www.usnews.com/news/business/articles/2016-03-08/blue-origin-planning-human-test-flights-to-space-by-2017

Bezos, who wants to put hotels and amusement parks in space with colonies of 2 to 3 million people [...]

» https://en.wikipedia.org/wiki/Jeff_Bezos

> Martinez, Amy (March 31, 2012). "Amazon.com's Bezos invests in space travel, time". *The Seattle Times*. Retrieved August 10, 2013.

REFERENCED LEADER'S SOURCES and ADDITIONAL INFORMATION

» http://articles.latimes.com/2012/apr/07/business/la-fi-bezos-20120407

"Go where no man but William Shatner has gone before"

» https://en.wikipedia.org/wiki/Where_no_man_has_gone_before

Page 169

Robin Williams **(July 21, 1951 – August 11, 2014)** [...] Despite his bouts of rehab, marriages and heart problems, Robin Williams seemed happy, spontaneous and alive with hilarity. But his last act was one of suicide. It conjures up images of a man with the desperate need to die, so desperate that he would use a belt to strangle himself. [...]Robin Williams was a senior with several diseases and a dying body...

» https://en.wikipedia.org/wiki/Robin_Williams#Death

    » Itzkoff, Dave; Fitzsimmons, Emma G.; Weber, Bruce (August 11, 2014). "Robin Williams, Oscar-Winning Comedian, Dies at 63". *The New York Times*. Retrieved August 11, 2014.

    » Soo Youn. "Robin Williams: Autopsy Confirms Death by Suicide". *The Hollywood Reporter*. Retrieved February 28, 2015.

» http://www.newyorker.com/culture/cultural-comment/suicide-crime-loneliness

» http://www.nydailynews.com/entertainment/gossip/robin-williams-widow-opens-living-nightmare-article-1.2421589

» "In an emotional interview last month, Susan said her husband was "living in a nightmare" in his final weeks because of Lewy Body Dementia, which he was diagnosed with after taking his life in August 2014. He was diagnosed with Parkinson's disease three months before."

"The reasonable man adapts himself to the world; the unreasonable one persists in trying to adapt the world to himself. Therefore all progress depends on the unreasonable man." ~George Bernard Shaw

» https://en.wikiquote.org/wiki/George_Bernard_Shaw

» http://www.goodreads.com/author/quotes/5217.George_Bernard_Shaw

Page 170

That old saying, "If the mountain won't come to Muhammad then Muhammad must go to the mountain," published back in the 1600's in a book of English proverbs.

» https://en.wikiquote.org/wiki/List_of_misquotations

  » Often attributed to the prophet Muhammad but there's no evidence that he actually said this. This phrase actually originates in a retelling of the story of Muhammad by Francis Bacon in 1625. translates, "If one's will does not prevail, one must submit to an alternative."

CPSIA information can be obtained
at www.ICGtesting.com
Printed in the USA
FSOW02n0958090916
24689FS